European Union

London: H M S O

Researched and written by Reference Services, Central Office of Information.

© Crown copyright 1994

Applications for reproduction should be made to HMSO.

First published 1994

ISBN 0 11 701794 9

HMSO publications are available from:

HMSO Publications Centre
(Mail, fax and telephone orders only)
PO Box 276, London SW8 5DT
Telephone orders 071-873 9090
General enquiries 071-873 0011
(queuing system in operation for both numbers)
Fax orders 071-873 8200

HMSO Bookshops
49 High Holborn, London WC1V 6HB   071-873 0011
Fax 071-873 8200 (counter service only)
258 Broad Street, Birmingham B1 2HE   021-643 3740   Fax 021-643 6510
33 Wine Street, Bristol BS1 2BQ   0272 264306   Fax 0272 294515
9-21 Princess Street, Manchester M60 8AS   061-834 7201   Fax 061-833 0634
16 Arthur Street, Belfast BT1 4GD   0232 238451   Fax 0232 235401
71 Lothian Road, Edinburgh EH3 9AZ   031-228 4181   Fax 031-229 2734

HMSO's Accredited Agents
(see Yellow Pages)

and through good booksellers

Contents

Acknowledgments	iv
Introduction	1
How the Community Works	2
The Rome Treaty	3
Single European Act	3
Community Institutions	4
European Monetary System	9
Community Structural Funds	9
European Investment Bank	10
International Agreements	10
Political Co-operation	11
The Maastricht Treaty	12
General Objectives	13
Subsidiarity	15
Citizenship of the Union	17
Community Institutions	18
General Economic Policy	23
Monetary Union	24
The Community Budget	29
Common Commercial Policy	30
Other Community Policies	30
Social Policy	36
Common Foreign and Security Policy	38
Justice and Home Affairs	43
Ratification	46
Extracts from House of Commons Debates on the Treaty	49
Further Reading	91
Abbreviations	92
Index	93

Acknowledgments

The Central Office of Information would like to thank the Foreign and Commonwealth Office for their help in compiling this book.

Cover Photograph Credit

European Commission

Introduction

Britain[1] is a committed member of the European Union and took an active part in the negotiation of the Maastricht Treaty, which came into force on 1 November 1993 following ratification by Britain and the other 11 member states. The Treaty created the European Union, whose three pillars are:

—the European Community;

—intergovernmental co-operation on a common foreign and security policy; and

—intergovernmental co-operation in the fields of justice and home affairs.

This book starts with a brief description of the way in which the Community and Union work. The main part of the text is a factual summary of the main provisions of the Treaty. The book concludes with edited extracts from speeches made in the House of Commons by Government and official Opposition spokesmen during debates on the Treaty.

---

[1] The term 'Britain' is used in this book to mean the United Kingdom of Great Britain and Northern Ireland; 'Great Britain' comprises England, Wales and Scotland.

How the Community Works

Following the disastrous experience of the Second World War, efforts were made by countries in Western Europe to co-operate to ensure that this would not be repeated. Approaches differed, Britain and some other countries favouring intergovernmental arrangements through organisations like the Council of Europe, established in 1949, and others wanting progress towards a federal Europe.

Because of dissatisfaction with purely intergovernmental arrangements, a supranational authority in the shape of the European Coal and Steel Community was created in 1952 under the 1951 Treaty of Paris, signed by Belgium, France, the Federal Republic of Germany, Italy, Luxembourg and The Netherlands. The Paris Treaty provided for the creation of a common market for coal and steel and measures to promote expansion and modernisation of production.

In 1957 the same six countries signed the Treaty of Rome which set up the European Economic Community. At the same time they signed another treaty establishing the European Atomic Energy Community (EURATOM).

Britain, together with Denmark and the Irish Republic, joined the three Communities in 1973, followed by Greece in 1981 and Spain and Portugal in 1986, bringing the total membership to 12. In 1993 member states started enlargement negotiations with Austria, Finland, Norway and Sweden.

In 1986 the Treaty of Rome was amended by the Single European Act. Further amendments were set out by the Maastricht

Treaty agreed by the European Council in December 1991 and signed by Community foreign ministers in February 1992.

The Rome Treaty

The Rome Treaty defines the Community's aims as the harmonious development of economic activities, balanced economic expansion and a rise in the standard of living. The main policies set out in the Treaty are:

—the elimination of customs duties between member states and of quantitative restrictions on the movement of goods;

—a common external tariff and a common commercial policy towards other countries;

—the adoption of common agricultural and fishing policies;

—free movement of people, services and capital between member states;

—the creation of a Social Fund to improve job opportunities;

—the establishment of a European Investment Bank to facilitate economic expansion; and

—the association of overseas developing countries with the Community in order to increase trade and economic and social development.

Single European Act

The Single European Act came into effect in July 1987 after ratification by all the member states. It provided for:

—the completion of the single European market in goods and services by the end of 1992;

—an improved co-operation procedure to enable the European Parliament to play a more active role in decisions on the internal market;

—the inclusion of provisions concerning collaboration in research and development and in environment policy; and

—formalisation and strengthening of co-operation on foreign policy issues.

The British Government took an active role in negotiating the main provisions of the Single European Act and welcomed its ratification by all the member states.

Community Institutions

The main Community institutions are the Council of the European Union, the European Commission, the European Parliament, the European Court of Justice and the Court of Auditors.

Brussels is the permanent seat of the Commission and the Council. The European Parliament's seat is in Strasbourg. The Court of Justice and the Court of Auditors have their headquarters in Luxembourg, as does the European Investment Bank.

The Council of the European Union

It is the Council, not bureaucrats, that adopts and amends decisions on Community laws. Each Council consists of Government ministers from the 12 member states, accountable to their national parliaments and representing national interests on the subjects under discussion. On general political issues, member states' foreign ministers usually take the decisions. On other occasions member states are represented by specialist ministers; for instance, when environmental matters are discussed, the Council consists of environment ministers.

Many important decisions (for example, on taxation policy, voting rights and the financial system, where member states have important national interests to protect) can be taken only if there is unanimous agreement in the Council.

For certain other policy decisions, a system of qualified majority voting (QMV) is used. This is a system of votes weighted according to the size of member states. It gives ten votes each to Britain, France, Germany and Italy, eight to Spain, five each to Belgium, Greece, The Netherlands and Portugal, three each to Denmark and the Irish Republic and two to Luxembourg. A minimum of 54 votes out of the total of 76 is needed for a measure to be agreed. The use of QMV became more common under the Single European Act to pass measures designed to build a single market based on genuinely free trade.

Member states assume the Presidency of the Council in rotation every six months. The Presidency sets the agenda for the Council and chairs meetings. The Council meets when convened by its President on his or her initiative or at the request of one of its members or the Commission.

A committee, consisting of member states' permanent representatives (ambassadors) in Brussels, prepares the work of the Council and carries out tasks assigned to it by the Council, which is assisted by a general secretariat.

The European Council, which consists of Heads of State or Government of the member states and the President of the Commission, usually meets twice a year to give overall direction to the work of the European Union.

Government ministers report to the British Parliament on the outcome of Council meetings and also appear before parliamentary committees.

The Council of the European Union's regulations are binding on member states and directly applicable. Its directives are also binding but they allow national governments to decide on ways of carrying them out. The Council can issue decisions binding on those to whom they are addressed, whether member states, firms or private individuals. The Council's recommendations and opinions are not binding.

The European Commission
The European Commission puts forward legislative proposals for consideration by the Council. Once the Council has taken its decision, the Commission is required to ensure that it is put into effect. It also enforces European Community treaties, with specific powers in the areas of competition and state aids. In addition, the Commission manages Community policies like the Common Agricultural Policy and negotiates international trade agreements on behalf of the Community, acting on a mandate agreed by the Council. The Commission prepares a draft budget every year and this has to be approved by the Council and the European Parliament.

There are 17 Commissioners who are nominated by individual governments and appointed with the agreement of all member states. Two each come from Britain, France, Germany, Italy and Spain; the other seven member states have one each.

Commission members must be completely independent in the performance of their duties and not take instructions from any government or from any other body. Member states are obliged not to seek to influence the members of the Commission in the performance of their tasks.

The European Parliament

The European Parliament's members are directly elected every five years by the people in each member state. The seats are shared out between member states broadly according to population.

The 1992 Edinburgh European Council agreed to increase the size of the European Parliament to reflect, in particular, the growth in the German population from 61 million to nearly 80 million following unification in 1990.

From 1994 Britain will have 87 members—71 for England, eight for Scotland, five for Wales and three for Northern Ireland. Members in England, Scotland and Wales are elected by a simple majority system in single member constituencies. Northern Ireland is one constituency, its three members being elected on the single transferable vote system of proportional representation.

Of the other member states, Germany will have 99 members and France and Italy 87 each. Spain will have 64 and The Netherlands 31. Belgium, Greece and Portugal will have 25 each. Denmark will have 16 members, the Irish Republic 15 and Luxembourg 6.

The Parliament meets in Strasbourg, usually once a month (with the exception of August), for plenary sessions lasting five days. Additional shorter plenary sessions are held in Brussels. When the Parliament is not sitting, committee work takes place in Brussels.

The Parliament must be consulted about major Community decisions and, with the Council of the European Union, is responsible for setting the Community budget.

When a draft law is sent to it by the Council, the Parliament may:

—approve the draft;

—propose amendments; or

—reject it.

If the Parliament rejects the Council's position, the Council may readopt it or revise it by unanimity. In the case of Parliamentary amendments, the Commission reviews them and may issue a revised proposal which is sent to the Council, which may:

—adopt the revised proposal;

—adopt those Parliamentary amendments not approved by the Commission by unanimity; or

—amend the Commission's revised proposal by unanimity.

The Maastricht Treaty has increased some of the Parliament's powers (see p. 20).

New applications for European Union membership must receive the assent of an absolute majority of the Parliament's members, as must the conclusion of agreements with third countries establishing an association involving reciprocal agreements. Under the Community Treaties, the Parliament may remove the Commission from office by a two-thirds majority of votes cast in a vote of censure; it does not have the power to remove individual Commissioners.

European Court of Justice

The European Court of Justice interprets and adjudicates on Community law. It can, for instance, declare void an act of the Council or the Commission which infringes the Treaties. Court rulings must be applied in member states. There are 13 judges, one from each member state and one extra to ensure an uneven number. Six Advocates General advise the Court.

The Court sits in plenary session but may form chambers of three or five judges to undertake preparatory enquiries or adjudicate on particular categories of cases.

A Court of First Instance handles certain cases brought by individuals and companies in order to relieve the burden on the main Court.

Court of Auditors

The Court of Auditors is responsible for overseeing the implementation of the Community's budget. It helps to counter waste and fraud. The Court consists of one member from each state.

European Monetary System

The European Community's European Monetary System (EMS) consists of an exchange rate mechanism (ERM), the European Currency Unit (ECU) and credit facilities. The ECU is a basket of Community currencies, the currency of each member state being proportionally represented according to economic size. Each currency in the ERM has an agreed central exchange rate against the ECU which is used to establish bilateral central exchange rates with the other currencies.

All EMS member states deposit 20 per cent of their gold and dollar reserves with the European Monetary Co-operation Fund in return for ECUs of the same value which may be used to settle obligations arising from intervention in the foreign exchange markets between the central banks concerned.

Britain, although a member of the EMS since its inception, did not join the ERM until October 1990. It withdrew from the ERM in September 1992 following severe turmoil on the international money markets.

Community Structural Funds

The Community has three Structural Funds intended to support development in less prosperous regions. The Social Fund supports training and employment measures for long-term unemployed and young people. Infrastructure projects and support for industry, particularly small and medium-sized enterprises, are financed by the Regional Development Fund. Part of the Agricultural Guidance and Guarantee Fund is used to support agricultural restructuring and some rural development.

European Investment Bank

The European Investment Bank provides medium- and long-term loans at attractive rates for public and private capital investment projects designed to further the economic development of the Community's less favoured regions and to improve communications between member states.

The 1992 Edinburgh Summit agreed to establish a new lending facility within the Bank to finance infrastructure projects throughout the Community, especially in transport, energy and telecommunications. This was increased at the June 1993 Copenhagen summit to include lending to small and medium-sized enterprises and will be worth some £6,200 million.

International Agreements

Under the Rome Treaty, the Community is given competence to conclude international trade and economic agreements. Under this procedure, the Commission makes recommendations to the Council of the European Union, which authorises the Commission to open the necessary negotiations. The Council acts by qualified majority, with some important exceptions. Unanimity is required for agreements which establish an association between other states or international organisations, involving 'reciprocal rights and obligations, common action and special procedures'. The European Parliament is also involved (see p. 8).

Political Co-operation

The Single European Act committed member states to the intergovernmental process of European political co-operation under which they formulate and implement agreed positions on important international issues where they have common interests.

The Maastricht Treaty

The Treaty of Rome's signatories declared themselves 'determined to establish the foundations of an ever closer union among the peoples of Europe'. The nature of such a union has never been formally defined. Successive British governments have opposed the creation of a unitary or federal Europe in which national sovereignty would be submerged. In practice, European union has meant a step-by-step process of increased co-operation, building on existing policies and elaborating new ones within the framework of the Treaties.

The success of the single market programme opened up a debate in the Community about strengthening political, monetary and economic co-operation. Intensive negotiations on amendments to the Rome Treaty took place within two intergovernmental conferences throughout 1991. Britain's objective during the negotiations was to create a more effective and efficient Community while avoiding centralisation in Brussels or any weakening of British national political institutions. Final discussions took place at the European Council meeting in Maastricht in December 1991.

The Maastricht Treaty on European Union:

—enshrines the principle of subsidiarity which operates to limit the Community's involvement in national affairs;

—provides for movement towards economic or monetary union, depending on the extent to which member states' economies converge in terms of inflation, interest rates and other criteria set out in the Treaty;

— establishes new rights for European Community citizens, without affecting national citizenship;
— carefully defines the scope for Community activity in areas such as health policy, education, training and culture by setting out the sort of action the Community should undertake;
— facilitates existing Community action in areas like environment policy and development aid for poor countries;
— makes the Commission more accountable to the European Parliament, while extending the latter's role in European Community legislation;
— enables the European Court of Justice to clamp down on those member states who do not comply with its judgments; and
— helps build closer intergovernmental co-operation on foreign and security policy and justice/home affairs, outside the procedures of the Rome Treaty.

The Maastricht Treaty establishes the European Union, which embraces the three Communities and the two pillars of intergovernmental activity on common foreign and security policy and on justice/home affairs. It also substitutes the term 'European Community' for 'European Economic Community' in the Treaty of Rome, reflecting the fact that the Community deals with more than just economic issues.

General Objectives

The Maastricht Treaty states that the objectives of the European Union are to:
— promote balanced and sustainable economic progress through the creation of an area without internal frontiers, the strengthen-

ing of internal cohesion and the establishment of economic and monetary union;
—implement a common foreign and security policy which might in time lead to a common defence;
—strengthen the rights and interests of member states' nationals through the introduction of citizenship of the Union; and
—develop close co-operation on justice and home affairs.

Under the Treaty the European Council is responsible for providing impetus to the Union. It submits to the European Parliament a yearly written report on progress achieved by the Union which shall 'respect the national identities of its member states, whose systems of government are founded on the principles of democracy'.

The Treaty defines the activities of the European Community as:
—the elimination of customs duties and quantitative restrictions on the import and export of goods;
—the implementation of a common commercial policy;
—the formation of an internal market removing obstacles to the free movement of goods, people, services and capital between the member states;
—preventing the distortion of competition in the internal market, including the approximation of member states' laws in order that this market can function properly;
—the strengthening of industrial competitiveness;
—the promotion of research and technological development;
—the application of common policies regarding agriculture, fisheries, transport, the environment, consumer protection and development co-operation;

—encouragement for the establishment and development of trans-European networks;

—the strengthening of economic and social cohesion;

—providing contributions to health protection, quality education and training and member states' culture;

—the formulation of policies on energy, civil protection and tourism; and

—the association of overseas countries and territories in order to increase trade and jointly promote economic and social development.

The Treaty states that there should be close co-ordination of members states' economic policies. Community economic policy should be conducted 'in accordance with the principle of an open market economy with free competition'. This involves the irrevocable fixing of exchange rates, leading to the introduction of a single currency and a single monetary policy. Guiding principles of economic policy are stable prices, sound public finances and monetary conditions and a sustainable balance of payments.

Subsidiarity

The Treaty stresses that the Community should act within the limits of the powers conferred upon it. This means that the Community only has functions which member states choose to give it and that all other powers remain with national governments.

Article 3b states: 'In areas which do not fall within its exclusive competence, the Community shall take action, in accordance with the principle of subsidiarity, only if and in so far as the objectives of the proposed action cannot be sufficiently achieved by the member states and can therefore, by reason of the scale or effects of the proposed action, be better achieved by the Community.'

The Article adds: 'Any action by the Community shall not go beyond what is necessary to achieve the objectives of this Treaty.'

A member state can challenge any Commission proposal on grounds of subsidiarity and bring before the Court of Justice any Commission or Council action which, in its view, infringes the principle. The Court decides whether or not the principle has been breached.

Since the signature of the Treaty in February 1992, more work has been done to ensure that the Community acts in accordance with the subsidiarity principle. The 1992 Edinburgh summit conclusions stated that it allowed 'Community action to be expanded where circumstances so require, and conversely, to be restricted or discontinued where it is no longer justified'. According to new agreed guidelines, 'the Council must be satisfied that action at Community level would produce clear benefits by reason of its scale or effect compared with action at the level of the member states'. In addition, the Community has to consider whether 'the issue under consideration has transnational aspects which cannot be satisfactorily regulated by action by member states'.

The Edinburgh Summit conclusions also stressed that 'the Community should only take action involving harmonisation of national legislation, norms or standards where this is necessary to achieve the objectives of the Treaty'. Community action, moreover, 'should leave as much scope for national decision as possible, consistent with securing the aim of the measure and observing the requirements of the Treaty'.

The Edinburgh Summit agreed that the Council should ensure that Commission proposals accord with subsidiarity and that any decision on this is taken at the same time as any decision on the substance of the proposal. The Commission, too, has to ensure that its proposals are in line with the subsidiarity principle. In addition, the Commission has agreed to consult more widely before proposing legislation; this process could include consultation with all the member states and a more systematic use of consultation documents (green papers).

Citizenship of the Union

The Maastricht Treaty establishes the concept of citizenship of the European Union. This adds to, and does not replace, national citizenship. Under this every person holding the nationality of a member state becomes a Union citizen. The existing right to move and reside freely within the territory of the member states is confirmed. Under these Treaty provisions:

—Community nationals resident in another member state are able to vote and stand as a candidate in local elections there and in European Parliament elections under the same conditions as nationals of their state of residence;

—Citizens of the European Union have the right to petition the European Parliament;

—Union citizens have the right to complain about Community maladministration to a new Ombudsman; and

—Community nationals are entitled to diplomatic and consular protection by representatives of other Community governments in third states where their country is not represented.

Proposals to strengthen or add to these rights require unanimous agreement by the Council and adoption by member states in accordance with their constitutions. This requires an Act of Parliament in Britain.

Individual member states remain responsible for determining who is entitled to be a national in their state.

The Commission is obliged to provide regular reports to the Council and the European Parliament on the application of the provisions of this part of the Treaty. On this basis, the Council has the right to adopt provisions to strengthen or add to these rights.

Community Institutions

The Maastricht Treaty, building on the Treaty of Rome, makes a number of changes affecting the various Community institutions.

Council of the European Union

The main Treaty provisions affecting the Council are:

— greater use of qualified majority voting;

— the need to take account of subsidiarity when taking decisions (see p. 15); and

— the intergovernmental arrangements for common policies on foreign and security matters and on justice/home affairs (see p. 38–45).

European Commission

The Maastricht Treaty confirms the existing number of Commission members and gives the European Parliament more powers concerning them. The President and the other members are subject as a body to a vote of approval by the European Parliament. Once approved by the Parliament, they are appointed by common agreement of the member states.

From 7 January 1995 the Commission's term of office will become co-terminous with that of the European Parliament and extended from four to five years. The Commission appointed for 1993 is serving a two-year term.

Court of Justice

The Court of Justice is given a new power to fine member states which do not comply with earlier Court judgments. Under the Treaty the Commission recommends the size of the fine, although the Court itself takes the final decision in the light of the circumstances of the case. This was a British proposal designed to strengthen the rule of law in the Community.

The Council, the Commission or individual member states can bring cases to the Court alleging misuse of powers or infringement of the Treaty or of any rule of law relating to its application. Actions can also be brought by the European Parliament. An action on infringement of the Treaty can take place only if the institution concerned has first been called upon to act. If, within two months, the institution has not defined its position, the action may be brought within a further period of two months.

The Court of Justice does not have jurisdiction over foreign/security or justice/home affairs matters; under the Treaty member states may, however, choose to give it jurisdiction to interpret specific conventions which they agree on justice/home affairs.

The Council is able by unanimity to expand the jurisdiction of the Court of First Instance without any need for a Treaty amendment. The aim of this provision, proposed by Britain, is to help reduce the Court's workload and delays to litigation.

Court of Auditors

Under the Treaty, the Court of Auditors is responsible for examining the accounts of all Community revenue and expenditure. Under new powers, the Court provides the European Parliament and the Council with a statement of assurance on the reliability of the accounts and the legality of underlying transactions. The Court is empowered to publish an annual report on the implementation of the Community budget.

Court members, states the Treaty, should be 'completely independent in the performance of their duties' and should not 'seek or take instructions from any government or from any other body'.

European Parliament

More powers for the European Parliament are set out in the Treaty:

Adoption of Community Legislation

Under Article 189b the Parliament can reject certain proposals by an overall majority under the so-called negative assent procedure. Policies affected by this provision include:

—free movement of workers;

—right of establishment;

—treatment of foreign nationals;

—mutual recognition of qualifications;

—education and culture;

—public health;

—consumer protection;

—guidelines for trans-European networks;

—research and development; and

—the environment.

Decision-taking under this provision of the Treaty starts with the Commission submitting a proposal to the Council and to the Parliament. The Council, acting by a qualified majority after obtaining the Parliament's opinion, adopts a common position which is communicated to the Parliament.

If the Parliament approves the common position within three months, or if the Parliament fails to act, the Council goes ahead with the measure. If, on the other hand, the Parliament indicates by an absolute majority of its members its intention to reject the common position, it must inform the Council immediately. The Council can convene a meeting of a conciliation committee, consisting of representatives of the Council and the Parliament, in order to exchange views. After this, the Parliament has the power to confirm, by an absolute majority of its members, its rejection of the common position; if it does so, the measure is not adopted by the Community.

The Parliament also has the power to propose amendments to the Council's common position; the amendments are sent to the Council, which can:

—approve them and adopt the legislation; or

—convene a meeting of the conciliation committee in the event of disagreement.

This committee is responsible for reaching agreement on a joint text. The Commission also takes part in the proceedings. If, within six weeks of its being convened, the committee approves a joint text, the Parliament and the Council have a further period of six weeks in which to adopt the legislation. If either fails to approve the legislation, it is not adopted. When taking this decision, the

Council acts by a qualified majority and the Parliament by an absolute majority of votes cast.

In some cases the conciliation committee may be unable to approve a joint text. If this does happen, the legislation does not become Community law unless the Council, acting by a qualified majority, confirms the common position adopted before the initiation of the conciliation procedure. If the Council does so, the legislation is adopted unless the Parliament rejects the text by an absolute majority of its members. In the latter case the legislation is not adopted.

Other New Powers

If it considers that new legislation is required, the Parliament, acting by a majority of its members, can request the Commission to submit proposals.

Provision is made for the Parliament to set up a temporary committee of enquiry to investigate alleged contraventions or maladministration in the implementation of Community law; this does not apply if the case is subject to legal proceedings. The decision to set up an enquiry is taken at the request of a quarter of the Parliament's members.

The Parliament has the right to appoint an Ombudsman to deal with complaints from people regarding maladministration in Community institutions; this does not apply to the Court of Justice or the Court of First Instance when acting in their judicial role. If the Ombudsman finds a case of maladministration, he or she refers the matter to the institution concerned, which must respond to the Ombudsman within three months. The Ombudsman then reports to the Parliament and the institution. The Treaty stresses that the Ombudsman 'shall be completely independent in the performance of his duties'. The Parliament is responsible for laying down regulations and general conditions governing the performance of the Ombudsman's duties; this is done after seeking an opinion from the Commission and with the approval of the Council acting by a qualified majority.

When the Commission's members and its President are nominated, they are subject as a body to a vote of approval by the Parliament.

Role of National Parliaments
Attached to the Treaty are two important declarations on the role of national parliaments. The first, a British proposal, encourages national parliaments to increase their contacts with the European Parliament and to develop a greater involvement in the activities of the European Union through, for example, the scrutiny of Commission proposals, as happens in Westminster. The second is a French proposal for a Conference of Parliaments consisting of representatives of the European Parliament and of national parliaments. This Conference is consulted on the main features of the European Union without prejudice to the powers of the European Parliament or the rights of national parliaments.

General Economic Policy

The Community is already committed to economic policy coordination. The Council of Economic and Finance Ministers (ECOFIN) considers an annual economic report by the Commission and is empowered to make policy recommendations to member states.

The Maastricht Treaty takes this process a step further by making provision for broad economic policy guidelines to be agreed by the European Council on a basis of consensus. ECOFIN compares member states' policies and performance against these guidelines. If the economic policies of a member state are inconsistent with the broad guidelines, or if they risk jeopardising the proper functioning of economic and monetary union, ECOFIN can make recommendations to the member state concerned; this can occur only on the basis of a qualified majority vote following a proposal from the Commission. Neither the guidelines nor the ECOFIN recommendations are legally binding on member states.

Monetary Union

A three-stage monetary union process is envisaged by the Treaty. Stage 1, including the completion of the internal market, is largely complete. Stage 2, beginning in January 1994, involves preparatory work and monetary policy co-ordination. Stage 3 comprises a move to fixed exchange rates, a single currency and the establishment of a European Central Bank. Britain is participating in the first two stages, but has a Treaty Protocol allowing Parliament to decide whether and when to join Stage 3.

Second Stage

During Stage 2, essential responsibility for economic and monetary policy remains with national governments and central banks. A European Monetary Institute (EMI) will be established in Frankfurt and managed by a council consisting of a President and the Governors of the national central banks, one of whom will be EMI Vice-President. The President is appointed by heads of state or Government.

The EMI will assume the functions of the existing Committee of Central Bank Governors and be responsible for technical preparations for Stage 3, including the introduction of a single monetary policy, and for offering non-binding opinions on the economic policies of member states. It will also:

—strengthen co-operation between national central banks;

—improve co-ordination of member states' monetary policies in order to ensure price stability;

—monitor the functioning of the EMS (see p. 9);

—take over the tasks of the European Monetary Co-operation Fund (see p. 9), which will be dissolved, and facilitate the use of the ECU (see p. 9); and

—supervise the technical preparation of ECU bank notes.

Budget Deficits
The Treaty states that during Stage 2 member states 'shall endeavour to avoid excessive budgetary deficits'. The Commission will monitor member states' budgetary situations and their stock of government debt with a view to identifying gross errors. If it considers that there is an excessive budget deficit in a member state, it can submit an opinion to the Council. The Council, acting by a qualified majority and having considered any observations by the member state concerned, will decide whether an excessive deficit exists, and if so, it can make non-binding recommendations to the member state concerned.

Member states who proceed to Stage 3 have to avoid excessive government budget deficits. If a member state fails to reduce the deficit, the Council may decide to give notice to the state to take measures to do so. If the state still fails to comply with the

Council's decision, the Council will be able, among other measures, to impose a fine and invite the European Investment Bank to reconsider its lending policy towards the state.

The Treaty also deals with the problem of member states who have serious balance of payments problems which threaten to jeopardise the working of the single market during Stage 2. The Commission may suggest measures to overcome such difficulties; if the action taken by the state, or the measures suggested by the Commission, turn out to be insufficient, the Commission can recommend the granting of mutual assistance to the member state concerned. The Council takes its decision by qualified majority voting.

During Stage 2, the Commission and the EMI will report to the Council of the European Union on the progress made by member states towards economic and monetary union. The Council has to assess which member states meet the necessary conditions for a single currency and whether a majority do so. It will recommend its findings to the European Council and the European Parliament will be consulted. The Council will take four 'convergence criteria' into account:

—average inflation over one year to be not more than 1.5 per cent above the rates in the three member states where it is lowest;

—average long-term interest rates over one year to be within two percentage points of the rates prevailing in, at most, the above three countries;

—no member state should have a budget deficit which the Council has formally designated as excessive; and

—a member state's currency would have to demonstrate successful membership for two years of the normal fluctuation band of the ERM without being devalued on that state's own initiative.

Additional factors to be considered will be the development of the ECU, the degree of market integration, unit labour costs and the balance of payments situation.

The European Council, acting by qualified majority, will, not later than 31 December 1996, decide whether the Community should enter Stage 3 of monetary union and, if so, will set the date. If the date for the beginning of Stage 3 has not been fixed by the end of 1997, it will begin on 1 January 1999; only those member states meeting the conditions for Stage 3 can be included.

Stage 3 of EMU
For the final stage of monetary union, to which Britain is not committed (see p. 28), the Treaty provides for the creation of a European System of Central Banks (ESCB) and a European Central Bank (ECB). The ESCB will consist of the ECB and the national central banks of the participating states. The system will be managed by the ECB's Governing Council, comprising an Executive Board, plus the national central bank governors of participating member states. The ECB Executive Board will consist of the President, Vice-President and four other members with relevant professional experience. These four will be nationals of member states participating in Stage 3 and will be appointed by the European Council.

The ECB's General Council will carry out certain tasks previously undertaken in Stage 2 by the EMI. In carrying out their duties under the Treaty, the ECB and the national central banks must be independent. The national central banks of member states not moving to Stage 3 will not be full members of the ECB or subject to its policies.

The primary duty of the ESCB will be to maintain price stability and support general Community economic policies. It will also be involved in:

—defining and implementing Community monetary policy;

—conducting foreign exchange operations;

—holding and managing official foreign reserves without prejudice to the management by member governments of foreign exchange working balances; and

—promoting the smooth operation of payment systems.

The ECB, which will take over the functions of the EMI, will be consulted upon any proposed Community act in its fields of competence. Similarly, national authorities will consult the ECB, which may submit opinions to Community institutions or national authorities.

The ECB will have the exclusive right to authorise the issue of bank notes within the Community. It and the national central banks will be able to issue such notes, which will be the only legal ones. Member states will have the right to issue coins subject to approval by the ECB of the volume of the issue. After consulting the ECB, the Council of the European Union will have the right to adopt measures designed to harmonise the denominations and specifications of coins to permit their smooth circulation within the Community.

The ECB may make binding regulations. It will be able to impose fines or penalty payments on undertakings for failure to comply with obligations under its regulations and decisions.

British Protocol on EMU
Britain has negotiated a Protocol to the Treaty which recognises that Britain 'shall not be obliged or committed to move to the third

stage of Economic and Monetary Union without a separate decision to do so by its government and Parliament'. This means that parts of the Treaty relating to Stage 3 of EMU do not apply to Britain, unless, of course, it chooses to join a single currency and satisfies the necessary conditions. In common with other member states not participating in Stage 3, the Bank of England will only be represented on the ECB's General Council (see p. 27) and will not have a seat on the ECB Governing Council's Executive Board. Denmark has a similar protocol.

The Community Budget

The Treaty states that, without prejudice to other revenue, the budget shall be financed wholly from the Community's revenue known as 'own resources'. Ways of raising Community revenue require unanimous approval by the Council of the European Union. On budgetary discipline, the Commission must show that its proposals are put forward with proper regard for their cost and affordability. Once the budget is agreed, the Commission must implement it and have regard to the principles of sound financial management. Acting unanimously, the Council has power to make regulations setting out the procedure for establishing and implementing the budget and for presenting and auditing accounts; it also decides the methods and procedures by which funds are made available to the Commission.

The European Parliament is given the power to examine the Community's accounts on the basis of observations made by the Court of Auditors. It can also request the Commission to report on any action it takes in response.

Largely at British instigation, the Treaty requires member states to take the same measures to combat fraud in the Community as they take to counter fraud affecting their own financial interests. Member states are required to co-ordinate anti-fraud measures by organising close and regular co-operation between the competent departments of their own administrations.

Common Commercial Policy

The Treaty largely codifies and updates existing provisions (see p. 10). There is no provision for European Parliament involvement in decisions on commercial policy.

Other Community Policies

There are new Treaty texts in several policy areas. In varying degrees these clarify, codify or extend Community competence. In every case there has already been activity by the Community or by the member states acting intergovernmentally.

Education, Vocational Training and Youth

The Treaty states that the Community should contribute to the development of quality education by encouraging co-operation between member states and supplementing their action. In so doing the Community has to respect fully 'the responsibility of the member states for the content of teaching and the organisation of education systems and their cultural and linguistic diversity'. The Treaty expressly excludes 'any harmonisation of the laws and regulations of the member states'.

Community action is to be aimed at:

—developing the teaching of member states' languages;

—encouraging the mobility of teachers and students and the mutual recognition of academic qualifications;

—promoting co-operation between educational establishments;

—encouraging more youth exchanges; and

—encouraging the development of distance learning.

Action by the Council is in the form of recommendations adopted by qualified majority.

The Treaty identifies five aims for Community activity on vocational training:

—retraining for industrial change;

—vocational integration and re-integration into the labour market;

—mobility of instructors and trainees;

—co-operation between training establishments and firms; and

—exchanges of information and experience.

Under these provisions the Council acts by qualified majority on a proposal from the Commission and adopts recommendations. As with education policy, the Treaty excludes any harmonisation of member states' laws and regulations in this area.

Culture

Article 128 states that the Community should contribute to 'the flowering of the cultures of the member states while respecting their national and regional diversity'; it excludes all harmonisation of member states' laws or regulations. Action is aimed at:

—improving knowledge of European culture;

—conserving cultural heritage of European significance;

—encouraging cultural exchanges; and

—supporting member states' actions on artistic and literary creation.

The Council acts unanimously on a proposal from the Commission and adopts recommendations.

Public Health

The Treaty supports Community action in ensuring a high level of human health protection. This is directed 'towards the prevention of diseases ... by promoting research into their causes and their transmission, as well as health information and education'. In undertaking this role, the Community and its member states are expected to co-operate with other countries and with international bodies such as the World Health Organisation. The Council, acting by a qualified majority on a proposal from the Commission, makes recommendations. Harmonisation of health service systems is excluded by the Treaty.

Trans-European Networks

In order to maximise the benefits of an area without internal frontiers, the Treaty states that the Community should set out guidelines for trans-European networks in transport, telecommunications and energy infrastructures: 'It shall take account in particular of the need to link island, landlocked and peripheral regions with the central regions of the Community.' One of the main aims is to support joint projects of common interest through feasibility studies, loan guarantees or interest rate subsidies, while taking into account potential economic viability.

The guidelines will be adopted by qualified majority voting after consultation with the new Committee of the Regions (see

p. 34) and will be subject to the European Parliament's negative assent procedure.

Industry
The Treaty pledges member states to ensure the existence of conditions for the competitiveness of the Community's industry. Action is designed to :

—help industry adjust to structural changes;

—encourage a favourable environment for co-operation between businesses; and

—foster improved exploitation of the industrial potential of innovation.

The Treaty encourages co-operation between member states on industrial competitiveness and provides for Community measures, adopted by unanimity in the Council, to be taken in support of member states' actions. Community action, however, must not distort competition.

Economic and Social Cohesion
Provision is made for strengthening economic and social cohesion with the aim of reducing regional disparities. This is done through Community institutions and the Structural Funds (see p. 9). The Treaty allows for the creation of a Cohesion Fund to help finance environment and transport projects in the poorer member states.

The Regional Development Fund, the Treaty confirms, 'is intended to help to redress the main regional imbalances in the Community through participation in the development and structural adjustments of regions whose development is lagging behind and in the conversion of declining industrial regions'.

The Treaty makes provision for the setting up of a Committee of the Regions to advise Community institutions on issues affecting regional interests. It must be consulted on new proposals in areas like education, culture, public health and trans-European networks. The committee will consist of representatives of regional and local bodies. Britain will have 24 of the 189 seats. Each member state decides how it should be represented. In 1993 the British Parliament decided that Britain's representatives should be drawn from elected local government representatives.

Research and Technological Development
An important Treaty objective, like that in the other Community treaties, is the strengthening of Community industry's scientific and technological bases to enable it to become more competitive. Article 130h says that the Community and the member states should co-ordinate their research activities to ensure that national policies and Community policy are mutually consistent.

Member states are committed to the creation of a framework programme setting out Community activities in this area. This is designed to:

—establish scientific and technological objectives; and

—fix the amounts and the detailed rules for Community financial participation in the programme.

Under the Treaty the framework programme is subject to the new negative assent procedure involving the European Parliament with the Council acting unanimously throughout the procedure. Specific programmes are adopted by qualified majority voting after consultations with the European Parliament. In addition the Council is empowered to determine rules for the participation of undertakings, research centres and universities in Community programmes.

The Environment

Community environment policy, states the Treaty, should contribute to:

— preserving, protecting and improving the quality of the environment;

— prudent and rational utilisation of natural resources; and

— promoting international measures to deal with regional or worldwide environmental problems.

Policy is based on the principles 'that preventive action should be taken, that environmental damage should as a priority be rectified at source and that the polluter should pay'.

A new objective contained in the Treaty is the promotion of measures at international level to deal with regional or worldwide environmental problems.

Most environment policy decisions are taken by the Council, acting by a qualified majority on a Commission proposal after obtaining the opinion of the European Parliament. This provision makes it easier to take urgent and effective action against major hazards. Unanimity is required in the Council for action regarding:

— fiscal measures;

— town and country planning;

— land use and management of water resources; and

— choice of energy sources.

Consumer Protection

The Treaty confirms the Community's commitment to 'the attainment of a high level of consumer protection' and to 'specific action which supports and supplements the policy pursued by the member states to protect the health, safety and economic interests of consumers and to provide adequate information to consumers'.

Any Community action is decided by qualified majority voting in the Council. Member states retain the right to adopt more stringent measures to protect consumers provided that these are compatible with the Treaty.

Help for Poor Countries

The Treaty codifies and expands existing practice in the Community's overseas development activities. Community policy is designed to foster:

— sustainable economic and social development;

— the smooth and gradual integration of developing countries into the world economy; and

— the campaign against poverty in the developing countries.

Community policy in this area should, the Treaty emphasises, promote democracy, the rule of law and human rights.

Article 130x states that the Community and the member states should 'co-ordinate their policies on development co-operation and … consult each other on their aid programmes…'.

Social Policy

The Treaty includes a Protocol and an agreement concluded between 11 member states on social policy. Britain is not committed to the agreement on the grounds that it might lead to arbitrary restrictions and unnecessary costs for employers, thereby damaging Community competitiveness in world markets. The British Government, however, believes that the Community, under the existing Treaty of Rome, has a role to play in supporting action to promote employment, labour flexibility and helping the unemployed back to work. It, therefore, supports Community action to improve training, raise health and safety standards and increase labour mobility.

Article 2 of the social policy agreement states that member states should support and complement each others' activities on:

—improving health and safety at work;

—working conditions;

—the information and consultation of workers; and

—equality between men and women with regard to job opportunities and treatment at work.

The Council is able to adopt by means of directives minimum requirements for gradual implementation. These are designed to avoid 'imposing administrative, financial and legal constraints in a way which would hold back the creation and development of small and medium-sized undertakings'.

The Council acts unanimously on a proposal from the Commission regarding:

—social security and social protection of workers;

—protection of workers where their employment contract is terminated;

—representation and collective defence of the interests of workers and employers, including co-determination; and

—conditions of employment for third country nationals legally residing in Community territory.

A member state can entrust management and labour, at their joint request, with the implementation of directives.

Member states are able to introduce more stringent protective measures compatible with the Treaty if they so desire.

Article 2 does not apply to pay, the right of association, the right to strike or the right to impose lock-outs.

Article 3 of the social policy agreement entrusts the Commission with the task of 'promoting the consultation of management and labour at Community level and shall take any relevant measure to facilitate their dialogue by ensuring balanced support for the parties'. To this end, the Commission consults management and labour before submitting social policy proposals. If, after such consultation, the Commission considers Community action is advisable, it consults management and labour on the content of the envisaged proposal. Management and labour forward to the Commission their opinions or, where appropriate, a recommendation.

Under Article 4 dialogue between management and labour at Community level can lead to contractual relations, including agreements.

Common Foreign and Security Policy

The Maastricht Treaty's provisions on a common foreign and security policy continue developments which have been taking place in European political co-operation. Obligations under the policy take effect in international law and not Community law; accordingly the Treaty excludes this area from the jurisdiction of the Court of Justice. Policy statements are made in the name of the European Union. The objectives are to:

—strengthen the security of the Union and its member states;

—safeguard the fundamental interests and independence of the European Union;

—preserve peace and strengthen international security in accordance with the United Nations Charter;

—promote international co-operation; and

—develop and consolidate democracy and the rule of law and respect for human rights.

Member states are committed to active and unreserved support for the Union's foreign and security policies, which are decided by the Council. Any member state can refer to the Council any question relating to foreign and security policy and may submit proposals for action. In cases requiring a rapid decision the Presidency convenes a meeting of the Council within 48 hours or earlier in the case of an emergency. The Commission is fully associated with the work carried out under the common foreign and security policy; it can submit proposals but cannot block agreement. Nor does it have the exclusive right of initiative or the watchdog role on implementation.

All significant decisions are taken by unanimity. There is provision for the Council to decide that certain decisions under joint action should be taken by a qualified majority; any decision to do this, however, is subject to unanimity, as is the initial decision to make any issue subject to joint action. Issues with defence implications are not subject to joint action and cannot be subject to qualified majority voting.

If a member state plans to adopt a national position or take national action in support of a joint action, it has to provide information in time to allow, if necessary, for prior consultations within the Council.

The Treaty differentiates between security and defence policy. It confirms that the Western European Union (WEU) is responsible for 'elaborating and implementing decisions and actions ... which have defence implications', although there is no obligation on members of the European Union to join the WEU. There is, however, a commitment to 'the eventual framing of a common defence policy, which might in time lead to a common defence'.

Maastricht Treaty provisions do not prejudice 'the specific character of the security and defence policy of certain member states and shall respect the obligations of certain member states under the North Atlantic Treaty and be compatible with the common security and defence policy established within that framework'.

The European Union is represented by the Presidency of the Council on foreign and security policy matters. The Presidency, and not the Commission, is responsible for the implementation of policy and expresses the views of the Union in international conferences and organisations. It is assisted in this, if necessary, by the previous and next member states to hold the Presidency (the EU Troika). The Commission is fully associated with these tasks.

Member states which are members of the UN Security Council concert their action and keep the other member states informed. Britain and France, which are permanent Security Council members, should in the execution of their UN functions 'ensure the defence of the position and interests of the Union, without prejudice to their responsibilities under the provisions of the United Nations Charter'.

The Treaty states that diplomatic and consular missions of the member states and the European Commission in third countries and at international conferences and delegations in international organisations should co-operate 'in ensuring that the common positions and common measures adopted by the Council are complied with and implemented'. The European Union, unlike the European Community, does not enjoy international legal personality. It cannot, for example, send or receive legations.

The Presidency is obliged to consult the European Parliament on the main aspects and basic choices of the common foreign and security policy and to ensure that the Parliament's views are duly taken into consideration. The Parliament can also make recommendations to the Council and it holds an annual debate on progress in implementing foreign and security policy.

A declaration annexed to the Treaty at the insistence of the British Government safeguards its right and that of other member states with dependent territories to represent their interests.

The Western European Union
A separate declaration was signed at Maastricht by member states of the Western European Union—Britain, Belgium, France, Germany, Italy, Luxembourg, The Netherlands, Portugal and Spain. The other Community member states were invited to become members of the WEU or observers; other European member states of the North Atlantic Treaty Organisation (NATO) were invited to become associate members of WEU. In November 1992 it was agreed that Greece would become a full WEU member, while Norway, Turkey and Iceland would be associate members and Denmark and the Irish Republic would be observers.

This Declaration states that WEU member states agree on the need to develop a genuine European security and defence identity and a greater European responsibility on defence matters. It also states that the WEU would be developed 'as the defence component of the European Union and as a means to strengthen the European pillar of the Atlantic Alliance'.[2] The WEU, said the signatories, was prepared at the request of the European Union to elaborate and implement decisions which had defence implications. At the same time the WEU would act in conformity with positions adopted in the NATO Alliance.

The WEU's operational role would be strengthened by:

—establishment of a WEU military planning cell;

—closer military co-operation which will be complementary to that of the NATO Alliance;

—meetings of WEU Chiefs of Defence Staff; and

—military units answerable to WEU.

The Declaration also commits WEU members to the aim of creating a European armaments agency. In December 1992 it was agreed that NATO's Independent European Programme Group (IEPG) would be merged with the WEU. Formed in 1976, the IEPG was set up to promote equipment co-operation and to work towards an open European defence equipment market based on cross-border competition. The IEPG has been replaced by the WEU's Western European Armaments Group, which is now the main European forum for consultations about armaments.

The seat of the WEU's Council and Secretariat has been transferred from London to Brussels.

Maastricht and NATO

NATO has welcomed the development of a European security and defence identity. NATO remains the main forum for consultation

---

[2] The term 'Atlantic Alliance' refers to NATO, created in 1949 to defend Europe against possible aggression by the then Soviet Union.

among its members on policies bearing on the security and defence commitments of Allies under the Washington Treaty, which set up NATO in 1949.

Justice and Home Affairs

For the purposes of achieving the free movement of people within the Community and other objectives, provisions for intergovernmental co-operation on justice and home affairs in the European Union are also set out in the Maastricht Treaty. These cover:

—asylum policy;

—rules governing the crossing by people of the member states' external borders;

—immigration policy;

—combating drug addiction;

—combating international fraud;

—judicial co-operation in civil matters;

—judicial co-operation in criminal matters;

—customs co-operation; and

—police action to prevent and combat terrorism, drug trafficking and other serious forms of international crime, including fraud.

Member states have to inform and consult each other within the Council of the European Union in order to co-ordinate their actions. In matters relating to judicial co-operation in criminal matters, customs co-operation and police co-operation, member states and not the Commission have the power to initiate Council discussions. In other areas, member states or the Commission can do so.

The Council can adopt joint positions and engage in joint action; member states can also enter into conventions. None of these are Community measures. The Council acts by unanimity. It can, however, decide that measures implementing joint action should be by qualified majority voting, but this decision must be made unanimously.

In general there is no jurisdiction for the European Court of Justice in the justice and home affairs policy area. However, member states can confer Community jurisdiction in relation to conventions adopted by member states. The first six items in the list on page 43 may be transferred into Community competence but only through unanimity in the Council and after ratification by all the member states in accordance with their constitutional requirements (an Act of Parliament in Britain). The last three items in the list cannot be transferred at all.

The Treaty provides for the creation of a Co-ordinating Committee of senior officials to give opinions to the Council and to prepare Council discussions on justice and home affairs. The European Commission is fully associated with the work.

The Presidency has to inform the European Parliament about Council discussions and to consult it on the main justice and home affairs activities. The Parliament can question the Council or make recommendations to it. In addition, the Parliament holds an annual debate on justice and home affairs.

Visa Policy
Articles 100c and 100d provide for the establishment of a common visa list—that is, a list of countries whose nationals need visas to enter the European Community member states—and a uniform format for visas to be agreed unanimously within the Community

framework. All other aspects of immigration policy, however, remain outside Community competence and are subjects for inter-governmental co-operation in the European Union.

Ratification

The Maastricht Treaty required ratification by all 12 member states before it could come into effect.

Three member states held referendums as part of this process in 1992. In the Irish Republic and in France voters approved the Treaty. In Denmark, however, there was a narrow majority against the Treaty in the referendum held in June 1992.

On 21 May 1992 the House of Commons gave a second reading to the Bill allowing Britain to ratify the Treaty. However, because of the Danish referendum result, the British Government postponed the Commons committee stages of the Bill.

As President of the Community, Britain convened a special meeting of the European Council at Birmingham on 16 October 1992. The Council's Declaration reaffirmed member states' commitment to the Maastricht Treaty while emphasising the need for Community decisions to be taken according to the subsidiary principle (see p. 15).

Through the autumn of 1992, discussions took place among member states on Danish concerns about the Treaty. The Danish Government indicated that it would hold a second referendum in the spring of 1993 if these concerns could be met by the Community.

The December 1992 Edinburgh summit agreed a set of arrangements to meet Denmark's concerns, including a legally binding Decision which interprets the provisions of the Treaty without modifying it or requiring re-ratification by member states. Under the Decision, Denmark's right not to take part in the third

The Foreign and Commonwealth Secretary, Douglas Hurd, signs the Maastricht Treaty in February 1992.

Youth exchanges between European countries are encouraged. Here, the Prime Minister, John Major, meets students on a visit to Britain.

Bavarian civil servants learning English at the British Council's teaching centre in Munich.

The European Union encourages cultural exchanges: Britain's Philharmonia Orchestra gives a regular series of concerts each year at the Châtelet Theatre in Paris.

One of 38 Channel Tunnel shuttle locomotives which will haul trains carrying heavy goods vehicles, coaches and cars between the British and French freight terminals.

Staffed and financed by the European Atomic Energy Community and 14 European nations, the Joint European Torus project at Abingdon, Oxfordshire, is designed to promote the use of nuclear fusion as a source of energy.

The European Parliament buildings in Strasbourg.

The Brussels headquarters of the European Commission.

stage of monetary union is confirmed. In addition, Denmark is not obliged to take part in any policies with defence implications. The Edinburgh conclusions also made it clear that, although the Maastricht Treaty gave nationals of member states additional rights, these did not take the place of national citizenship, which would be settled solely by reference to the national law of the member state concerned. On the basis of the arrangements agreed at Edinburgh, ratification of the Maastricht Treaty was approved by a second referendum in Denmark held in May 1993.

In early November 1992 the British Government declared that the remaining stages of its ratification Bill would be completed during the Parliamentary session ending in autumn 1993. The Bill duly completed its passage through Parliament and in July 1993 received Royal Assent making it law.

During its passage through Parliament, the Government accepted an official Opposition amendment which stated: 'This Act shall come into force only when the House of Commons has come to a resolution on a motion tabled by a Minister of the Crown considering the question of adopting the Protocol on Social Policy' (see p. 36).

Debates took place in both Houses of Parliament on this issue on 22 July 1993. Two motions were before the House of Commons. The Government motion took note of the Government's policy on the Maastricht Social Protocol while the Labour Opposition amendment called for the Treaty not to be ratified unless the Government adopted the Agreement on Social Policy annexed to the Protocol. The first Commons vote took place on the Labour amendment; it received 317 votes and the same number of votes were cast against. In these circumstances the Speaker of the House, Miss Betty Boothroyd, exercised a casting vote in support of the Government on the basis of precedent. The Government motion on the second vote was lost by 324 to 316.

Responding to this vote, the Prime Minister told the House that it would be invited to vote on a motion of confidence.

On 23 July a Commons debate took place on a Government motion which stated: 'That this House has confidence in the policy of Her Majesty's Government on the adoption of the Protocol on Social Policy.' This was approved by a majority of just over 40.

A legal challenge to the Government's intention to ratify the Treaty was then brought but, following its clear rejection by the Divisional Court, the applicant withdrew the action. The British Government accordingly deposited its instrument of ratification of the Treaty on 2 August 1993.

German ratification was delayed pending judgments to be made by the country's Constitutional Court in Karlsruhe. Following a successful outcome to the case, Germany ratified the Treaty on 13 October and it came into force on 1 November 1993.

Extracts from House of Commons Debates on the Treaty

Speech made by the Prime Minister, John Major, to the House of Commons on 20 November 1991

The European Council in Maastricht is set to decide issues which are crucial to the future of the European Community and to Britain's role as a leading member of it. This afternoon I would like to set out what is at stake, the parameters of what we can accept and also what we cannot accept.

I shall deal, first, with a misconception that is held by some of our Community partners. They believe that Britain may argue hard against many of the proposals—object to them and protest—but that then we shall sign up to whatever is on offer at the 59th minute of the 11th hour. I urge them not to make that misjudgment; it would be fatal.

The Government want to reach an agreement at Maastricht. We are negotiating for one. There is still some way to go and I hope that we will be successful, but it may be that a deal is genuinely unobtainable. If we do not reach an agreement, it will be a setback. So it must not be through misunderstanding, or misjudgment, and certainly not through bad faith. Therefore, this afternoon I will make our position clear

Community Membership

For historical, geographical and political reasons, the issue of membership of the European Community has been more controversial in Britain perhaps than in any other member state. We joined the Community late, and we joined a Community whose rules were drawn up by the original members and not by us. The structure of the Community's budget meant that only two countries—Britain and Germany—were net contributors. The common agricultural policy was designed to benefit those countries with small and often inefficient farmers. It took time, effort and controversy to redress some of those imbalances. My right hon Friend the Member for Finchley [Mrs Thatcher] secured a more equitable budget arrangement, and now we have started on the reform of the common agricultural policy.

Those issues have often obscured the benefits to Britain of the European Community. The first and perhaps overriding benefit is the contribution which the Community has made to democracy, stability and prosperity in post-war Europe. The Community is unique in having its own framework of law that is binding on member states. That framework of law is changing, not least to enable us to create the world's largest single market. Prior to the Single European Act, we were at a disadvantage. Britain had removed most of the barriers which stood in the way of countries wanting to export to us, but the reverse in no sense was the case. We often faced barriers to the export of our goods to other Community countries.

It is because of our membership of the Community that Nissan cars, made in Sunderland, can be sold freely in continental Europe. Seventy-five per cent of the Sunderland factory's production went for export last year.

It is because of Community law that we shall be able to sell our financial, banking and insurance services freely throughout the Community. It is thanks to the collective strength of the Community that we can negotiate a good deal for Britain in international trade negotiations with the United States and Japan.

Those are all positive advantages. They illustrate very clearly why the countries of the European Free Trade Association, none of them economic slouches, have just done a deal with the Community. That agreement gives them the benefits of the European single market. In exchange, they have had to accept our regulations and our standards without having any say in framing them. Most of them now want membership of the Community to give them that equal say in framing the Community's laws.

There are, in truth, only three ways of dealing with the Community: we can leave it, and no doubt we would survive, but we would be diminished in influence and in prosperity; we can stay in it grudgingly, in which case others will lead it; or we can play a leading role in it, and that is the right policy. It does not mean accepting every idea that is marketed with a European label. It does mean trying to build the sort of Europe that we believe in, and I will turn specifically to that in the course of my remarks. ...

At the Luxembourg European Council in June, draft texts on monetary union and political union were produced that had huge deficiencies but which did recognise many of our concerns. In September, a new Dutch text on political union appeared. That was quite unacceptable and we rejected it. It was withdrawn, and replaced a few days ago. These early texts have caused much alarm about proposals that this country would and could never have accepted.

Economic and Monetary Union
I will turn first to the treaty articles on economic and monetary union. The Treaty of Rome defines as its goal the achievement of 'an ever closer union among the peoples of Europe'. In 1972, the Heads of Government of the Community—and of Britain, Ireland

and Denmark, who were about to join—agreed the objective of the 'progressive realisation of Economic and Monetary Union'. That goal was enshrined in the preamble to the Single European Act. But these goals were never defined.

The treaty now before us envisages the realisation of economic and monetary union through the creation of a single European currency to replace the historic currencies and a European central bank to manage monetary policy.

In stage 1 the single market and single financial area will be completed; competition will be strengthened; capital movements liberalised and the greatest possible number of currencies will join the exchange rate mechanism of the European monetary system. The United Kingdom is fully committed to stage 1 which began on 1 July 1990. The substantive provisions of the treaty apply to the second and third stages of economic and monetary union. It is here that we begin to run into the areas of greatest difficulty and controversy in much of the negotiation before us.

In the second stage, the text proposes to establish a European monetary institute, essentially the present meeting of European central bank governors under another name. Its task would be to strengthen the co-operation between the member states' central banks and to promote the co-ordination of monetary policy. In stage 2 the European currency unit would be developed and hardened. During the whole of this period, monetary policy would remain entirely in the hands of member states. The European monetary institute would have a consultative and advisory role, and that alone.

The present stage envisages that, before the end of 1996, the member states of the Community would take stock, in the Economic and Finance Council and in the European Council, and reach a decision as to whether to move to the final stage of economic and monetary union. A crucial element in the decision whether or not to move to stage 3 would be the economic convergence of the member states. We were the first country to argue that convergence was vital before monetary union could even become a possibility. That view is now accepted by our partners. The latest text sets out strict convergence criteria on inflation, on interest rates, on successful membership of the narrow band of the exchange rate mechanism and on the avoidance of excessive budget deficits.

The Council of Ministers would decide who has met the conditions, and the European Council would decide unanimously whether or not the conditions were right for a move to stage 3. We believe that there should be at least eight member states ready to move to stage 3 before that step could be taken.

Our insistence that there should be no imposition of a single currency is well known: by that we mean that we cannot commit ourselves now to entry at a later date as a result of the treaty. We are therefore insisting that there must be a provision in the treaty giving us the right, quite separately from any European Council decision, to decide for ourselves whether or not to move to stage 3. That decision can be taken only by this House.

That means that, even if the requisite majority of member states decide to embrace full economic and monetary union with a single currency and a single central bank, Britain will not be obliged to do so. Whether to join—not just when to join—will be matters of separate decision by Government and by Parliament. Nothing in the treaty that I sign will bind us now to the decision that we must take then. Nothing in the treaty that I sign now will bind us then because at this stage we cannot know what the circumstances then will be and whether it will be in the economic interests of this country to take part. . . .

One of the most sensitive issues in this debate is the conduct of the United Kingdom's fiscal policy—the powers to tax, borrow and spend. It is common ground that excessive budget deficits should be avoided and that the absence of such deficits should be a convergence condition for moving to stage 3. It is also agreed that there should be no legally binding budget deficit ceilings and sanctions in stage 2.

For stage 2, the treaty would provide for a formal process whereby the ECOFIN Council can, on the basis of a Commission report, examine any state's economic policy and budgetary position. If it finds a budget deficit to be excessive, it can make non-binding policy recommendations. While the arrangements for prompting a Commission report would be an innovation in the text, the other powers of examination and recommendation are not. The Council can do that now—and it does. ...

Where we part company from some other member states is on stage 3. The Dutch draft treaty provides the ECOFIN Council with legally binding powers backed up by sanctions to require a member state to reduce its deficit. We consider that there is no better sanction than the market, and will continue so to argue in the intergovernmental conference.

There are some hon. Members who say—and I respect the feeling behind it—that the creation of a single currency and a European central bank should be blocked now. They believe that, if it is not, the pressures on us to join at a later stage will be irresistible. I am not of their view. It is true that, technically, we could block the adoption of an economic and monetary union treaty in its present form—that is, as an amendment to the treaty of Rome. What we could not do is to prevent some or all of the other 11 member states making a separate treaty on their own outside the treaty of Rome. ...

... Therefore, I do not believe that it would be right to block the treaty on economic and monetary union, provided that it contains within it the conditions that could make such a union a success. Nor is it necessary to do so to safeguard our own interests. For the text gives this country the crucial provision that we need, which means that we can decide at a time of our own choosing whether to join or not. ...

If the convergence conditions set out in the draft treaty are not met, we would certainly not wish to be part of an economic and monetary union with a single currency. But if they are met, our successors may wish to take a different view. A single currency could be the means of safeguarding anti-inflationary policies for the whole of the European Community. That would be a great prize. But the House knows that there is a price to pay for that prize. The price is that it would take from national Governments the control of monetary policy. That would be a very significant political and economic step for Britain to take. We cannot take that step now. But nor should we exclude it.

We have in front of us not, as it has been described, an opt-out clause but a clause that we have secured which enables us to opt in—if we wish, when we wish, and in conditions that we judge to be right. I believe that we should keep open that option and not foreclose it now.

Political Union

In many respects the treaty on political union poses starker problems. We are committed under the treaty of Rome to 'ever closer union among the peoples of Europe'. Under the Single European Act the member states of the Community agreed 'to transform relations as a whole among their states into a European union'. The purpose of the new treaty text is to define what political union means in practical, legal terms.

For many of our Community partners the definitions are not as important as they are for us. For many of them the diminution of the power of national Governments and national Parliaments is not an issue. They accept the idea of a European federation. We have never done so. When we joined, we accepted that Community law would take precedence over national law. But for that very reason we have always been concerned about the scope of Community law—precisely because it took precedence. In these negotiations we have shown ourselves ready to discuss individual changes in the role of the Community where these are in the national interest. But we are not prepared to accept wholesale changes in the nature of the Community which would lead it towards an unacceptable dominance over our national life. . . .

It is against that background that we approach the political union treaty with its implications for our national sovereignty. Unlike the provisions on economic and monetary union, these provisions can be adopted only if all 12 member states and their Parliaments agree. That safeguard is there to be used if it needs to be used.

There are many definitions of what federation means, but to most people in this country the notion of a federal Europe leads over time to a European Government and Parliament with full legislative powers, to which national Governments and Parliaments are subordinate. I do not believe that that is a road down which the country would wish to go. We will not therefore accept a treaty which describes the Community as having a federal vocation. Such a Community will not succeed.

Let me set out the main elements of the political union treaty, and our attitude to them. First of all is the treaty's structure. The first Dutch text in September brought all the elements of the treaty under a single structure—a unitary structure. That would have brought foreign policy, defence policy, interior policy and justice policy under the treaty of Rome and within the jurisdiction of the European Court of Justice. It would have been a massive stride towards a centralised federal structure.

Such a treaty may be popular with some of our European partners, but it is unthinkable for us. We made that clear, and those provisions have now been withdrawn.

The new treaty text would create what have become known as separate pillars. Some elements of our co-operation with our Community partners will come with the existing framework of Community law. Other elements of co-operation—notably on foreign and security policy, and against crime and terrorism—would be conducted on an intergovernmental basis. So, too, would co-operation in dealing with immigration and asylum. Those elements would be outside the treaty of Rome and outside the jurisdiction of the European Court of Justice. This means that there would be no supra-national authority to adjudicate on the decisions taken by member states.

Those changes are welcome. The countries of the European Community would be able to co-operate within a legal framework. But the European Court would not be involved; the Commission would not have the sole right to make proposals. Those changes represent a significant step forward towards practical, more flexible arrangements.

We began co-operation in foreign policy, security and defence on an intergovernmental treaty basis, and we did so as a result of the Single European Act. Co-operation in foreign policy with our partners in the Community is in the interests of this country. On most issues we carry more clout collectively than we would alone. It has therefore been a successful policy.

Joint Action
Under the Single European Act, we strengthened our co-operation by introducing the concept of joint action. That will continue under the new treaty. The text proposes that joint action, once determined by consensus, would be binding on all member states. Decisions on what should constitute joint action would be taken by unanimity, but it is proposed that detailed decisions, putting a decision of principle into practice, would be taken by a majority of member states. ...

I see merit in joint action and in that joint action being carried out by member states. For example, were we to take a decision, as 12 member states, to impose sanctions on a country it would be damaging for one member state to abrogate those sanctions unilaterally. In most areas it would be in our interest to work for joint action, but we cannot allow the search for joint action to inhibit our right to take separate national decisions essential for the pursuit of our foreign policy. Where we can act together we will do so. Where we need to act on our own we must be free to do so. Even where joint action has been agreed, there must be provision for a member state to act separately and unilaterally if it decided that its vital interests required it to do so. ...

Defence
On defence, the position is clear. We have in NATO the means of our defence. At the recent summit all the members of NATO were clear that we must do nothing to call in question the continuing American and Canadian presence in Europe. Europe should

undoubtedly do more for its own defence, but we do not need to invent a new structure for that to happen. We need to develop a policy that is consistent with our existing obligations and arrangements through NATO and the Western European Union.

It is for that reason that Britain and Italy put forward proposals which would build up the WEU, not as the European alternative to NATO, but as the European pillar of NATO. We would establish close links between the WEU and the European Union. We can discuss security issues in the European Council, but we cannot accept a situation in which the European Community would effectively set up a competing security structure....

We must not get into the habit of thinking that all European development has to take place through the European Community. I know that there are many in Europe who want to set everything in a Community legal framework, for fear that if they do not old nationalisms may reassert themselves. But that is not our view. We want to work more closely with our partners, but that co-operation does not always have to be in the same fixed framework. We have to find patterns of co-operation which work, and that may frequently be on an intergovernmental basis rather than in a full Community framework....

European Parliament

The role of the European Parliament is one of the most difficult issues in the development of the Community. There are widely differing views about it. Some believe that it should have the power to initiate legislation. We do not believe that. Many member states would like to give the European Parliament an effective power of co-decision, to make it an equal partner with the Council in determining Community law. We cannot agree to that. The Council of

Ministers, whose members are answerable to their national Parliaments, must be the body which ultimately determines the Community's laws and policies. But the European Parliament is elected. From its inception it has had the power to block the budget, sack the Commission, to propose amendments to Community legislation, and to give assent to certain international agreements. Its powers were increased by the Single European Act. . . .

...The Government would like to see the European Parliament given a greater role in monitoring the Commission and in scrutinising its role as the implementing authority of Council decisions. The Parliament should have a greater role in auditing the Community's expenditure. We would be willing to see the Parliament's links with the citizens who elected it strengthened through the appointment of a Community ombudsman directly answerable to the Parliament.

The European Parliament already has the power to dismiss the Commission. We are willing to see it take a greater role by approving the appointment of the Commission, although we do not think it right to give the Parliament the power of dismissing individual Commissioners. Those who favour the idea argue that it would lead to greater efficiency within the Commission. I am more inclined to believe that it would be likely to lead to a witch hunt against those Commissioners who carry out their duties without fear or favour. . . .

Wider Europe
Our overriding aim must remain democracy, stability and prosperity in Europe, but our responsibility is now wider than just to the existing members of the Community. It must also be to all the other European countries which are now returning to democracy for the first time in 50 years. Our door must be open to them.

We must prepare for the day when the EFTA countries in the north of Europe and the new democracies in the east of Europe want to become part of the Community. When they are economically ready to join the Community we must be ready to accept them; and we must tell them so now.

We can now plan for a European Community stretching north to the Baltic and east to the Urals—a Community that embraces the free market principles that are at the heart of the treaty of Rome. Such a Europe would be more than an economic entity.

It would not only guarantee prosperity, but would underpin democracy. It would put an end to centuries of mistrust, suspicion and war. It would secure a lasting peace across the whole of our continent. I believe that that is a Europe worth building and worth making sacrifices for. That is the Europe for which I shall argue at Maastricht.

Speech made by the then Leader of the Opposition, Neil Kinnock, to the House of Commons on 20 November 1991

The background to this debate, and clearly the cause of this debate, involves the great change—or different kinds of change—taking place across the continent of Europe and within the European Community. The basic question at issue in the debate is whether the United Kingdom is to be carried along in the wake of those changes or to be a driving force for change. It is essential that our country takes a lead. That is the only way to exert the decisive influence over the direction and nature of the economic, political and social development under way in Europe. The British people know that; they are well aware of the dangers of Britain being in a second division in Europe, and they do not want to be left behind.

Positive Approach
The need for an active and positive approach to change is well understood by Governments in the rest of the Community. They recognise the reality of the economic interdependence that now exists and which will be intensified by the completion of the single market. As a result, they are determined to build on that interdependence by moving towards economic and monetary union. They are clear about their objectives; they know what they want. This Government most certainly are not clear. ...

The Government must ... stop trying to persuade themselves or the country that some sort of semi-detached arrangement can be made that will serve Britain's interests—there is no such arrangement. Anyone who thinks there is should simply consider what our country's position would be if our neighbours and trading partners formed a monetary union and, even though economic convergence had been achieved, Britain stayed outside. ...

More immediately, before those years pass and there is any immediate prospect of monetary union, it must be recognised how vulnerable Britain would be if the Government's strategy were to avoid commitment to the process under way in the European Community. That is not a theoretical matter, but a practical issue. If a British Government continued, as a matter of policy, to stand apart from the process, would inward investors who need access to markets of the whole Community think of locating in a semi-detached country?...

...The Government should be negotiating to gain full recognition of the fact that monetary union and a single currency could work successfully only if there were convergence in the real economic performance of countries: convergence in terms of growth and employment, as well as in terms of inflation and interest rates. No one can be satisfied with the present position. British and

German inflation rates have moved together, but the German economy is growing at a rate of 3.5 per cent, while the British economy is in recession and shrinking by 2.5 per cent. Real convergence would mean similar and sustained growth rates, as well as similar inflation rates. ...

The Government claim that, whenever decisions are taken at Community level, they are the actions of bureaucratic and unaccountable members or agents of the Commission who are trying to push their way into every nook and cranny of national life. It is true that the Commission has great powers that have been ceded by Governments and Parliaments—powers that will not be reclaimed by Governments and Parliaments. All the more reason, therefore, to make changes to address the resulting democratic deficit by ensuring that the Commission is held more effectively to account by the European Parliament, which is elected by the people in every Community country. ...

Evolution of the Community

In the European circumstances, which are still volatile—sometimes tragically so—the Community has inevitably and increasingly become the centre of political and economic development in the entire continent. The evolution of the Community is continuing, both with the European Free Trade Association countries and with the new democracies of eastern and central Europe. That change must be fostered. I was glad to hear the Prime Minister strongly confirm that today. Among the most important of the actions to be taken is the gradual development of associate membership and then, I hope, full membership for countries in eastern and central Europe, both to encourage economic advance and, vitally, to strengthen democracy.

The European Community now has a political identity that is in part being forged by the efforts of member states and in part by the movement of international events, especially in recent years. Some wish further to define that identity by adopting common foreign and security policies, with qualified majority voting. That, however, would produce a result which would probably be the opposite of the one that the proponents desire. It would weaken, not strengthen the Community and its ability to act. Co-operation and consensus, therefore, remain the most useful and reliable arrangement for Community foreign and security policies.

Europe now has more democracy, more freedom and more potential for economic, social and cultural advance than ever before in its history, but we know that if that potential is to be fulfilled it cannot be left to chance. That is why we have put forward policies to promote efficiency and growth, opportunity and social justice. They are all essential components in the development of a Europe that is not only a market for its producers but a genuine community for all its people. Developing that market, building that community, is the future for Britain in Europe.

Report given by John Major to the House of Commons on 11 December 1991 regarding the outcome of the Maastricht negotiations

With permission, Mr Speaker, I should like to make a statement on the European Council in Maastricht which I attended with my right hon. Friends the Foreign Secretary and the Chancellor of the Exchequer.

The European Council has reached agreement on a treaty on European union. The relevant texts have been deposited along with the presidency conclusions. The House will be invited to debate the outcome next week.

Let me set out the main provisions of the agreements we reached.

The treaty covers economic and monetary union and political union. It follows the structure for which the United Kingdom has consistently argued.

The treaty creates a new legal framework for co-operation between member states in foreign and security policy and in the fight against international crime. That co-operation will take place on an intergovernmental basis outside the treaty of Rome. That means that the Commission will not have the sole right of initiative and the European Court will have no jurisdiction.

On defence, we have agreed a framework for co-operation in which the primacy of the Atlantic alliance has been confirmed and the role of the Western European Union has been enhanced.

As the House knows, there was strong pressure over many months for all aspects of co-operation to come within European Community competence. That was not acceptable to this country. Instead, an alternative route to European co-operation has been opened up. I believe that this will be seen as an increasingly significant development as the Community opens its doors to new members, and more flexible structures are required.

Single Currency

I turn now to the main features of the text. The treaty provides for the possibility that member states will wish to adopt a single currency later this decade, but they can do so only if they meet strict convergence conditions—conditions for which the British

Government have pressed from the outset. These cover inflation, budget deficits, exchange rate stability and long-term interest rates.

A single currency may come into being in 1997, but only if a minimum of seven countries meet the convergence conditions, and eight of the Twelve vote in favour. The treaty lays down that a single currency will come into being by 1999, but only if those convergence conditions are met and only for those countries which meet them. It is therefore highly uncertain when such a currency will be created and which countries it will cover.

In the House on 20 November, I said that there must be a provision giving the United Kingdom the right to decide for ourselves whether or not to move to stage 3. That requirement has been secured. It is set out in a legally binding protocol which forms an integral part of the treaty. The protocol was drafted by the United Kingdom and fully protects the position of this House. The effect of the protocol is as follows. We have exactly the same option to join a single currency at the same time as other member states if we wish. We shall be involved in all the decisions. But, unlike other Governments, we have not bound ourselves to join regardless of whether it makes economic or political sense.

Intergovernmental Co-operation
The treaty text on political union provides for enhanced intergovernmental co-operation on foreign and security policy, on defence policy and in the fight against terrorism, drug trafficking and other crimes.

International crime knows no frontiers. Terrorists and other criminals must not be allowed to escape justice or to retire abroad with the proceeds of their crime. This text gives us a new basis for co-operation with our partners in bringing these criminals to justice.

The text provides for joint action in foreign policy, building on what was already agreed in the Single European Act. But, as I told the House on 20 November, if Britain needs to act on its own, it must be free to do so. The treaty meets that requirement. Joint action can take place only if we agree. Where there is no joint action, each member state is entirely free to act on its own. If, after joint action has been agreed, a member state needs to take its own measures to meet changed circumstances, it may do so.

There was pressure from other member states to take foreign policy decisions by majority voting. I was not prepared to agree that Britain could be out-voted on any substantive issue of foreign policy. Some of our partners also sought to draw a distinction between decisions of principle, where unanimity would apply, and implementing decisions which could be subject to majority voting. No one was able to explain how that distinction would work. I told the European Council that, if such occasions did arise, we should consider the case for majority voting on its merits. The treaty reflects our view. It provides that the Council may, but only by unanimity, designate certain decisions to be taken by qualified majority voting. But we cannot be forced to subject our foreign policy to the will of other member states. We have, in fact, preserved unanimity for all decisions where we decide that we need it.

We are agreed that Europe must do more for its own defence. We should build up the Western European Union as the defence pillar of the European Union. But the treaty embodies the view set out in the Anglo-Italian proposal two months ago, and endorsed at last month's summit of the North Atlantic Treaty Organisation that whatever we do at European level must be compatible with NATO. The WEU must in no way be subordinate to the European Council. It is not. We have avoided the danger of setting up defence structures which would compete with NATO. We have created a framework in which Europe can develop its defence role in a way which complements the American presence in Europe and does not put it at risk.

The Citizen

In these negotiations, we put forward a series of proposals designed to be of direct benefit to the European citizen. All of them were accepted. The Community has agreed to increase the accountability of European Community institutions; to strengthen the European Parliament's financial control over the Commission; to allow the European Parliament to investigate maladministration and to appoint a Community ombudsman accessible to all Community citizens; to build up the role of the Court of Auditors, which becomes an institution of the Community; and to ensure compliance with Community obligations by giving the European Court of Justice power to impose fines on Governments who sign directives but subsequently do not implement them.

Powers of European Parliament

We wanted—and secured—a sensible enhancement of the role of the European Parliament. We did not accept the proposal made by other member states for a power of co-decision between the Parliament and the Council. As I told the House on 20 November, the Council of Ministers must be the body that ultimately determines the Community's laws and policies. I also said then that we were prepared to consider some blocking power for the European Parliament. That has now been agreed. The treaty sets up, in a limited number of areas, a conciliation procedure where there is disagreement between the Council and Parliament. In the last analysis, the Parliament would be able to block a decision in those areas, but only if an absolute majority of its members turned out to vote the proposal down.

Community Competence
The House has been rightly concerned at the creeping extension of Community competence over the last few years. The Commission has often brought forward proposals using a dubious legal base, and the Council has found it difficult to halt that practice in the European Court. We have taken significant steps to deal with that problem.

First, the structure of the treaty puts the issues of foreign and security policy, interior and justice matters and defence policy beyond the reach of the Commission and the European Court. Second, the treaty itself embodies the vital principle of 'subsidiarity', making it clear the Community should only be involved in decisions which cannot more effectively be taken at national level. Third, in some areas—notably health protection, educational exchanges, vocational training and culture—we have defined Community competence clearly for the first time. Fourth, there will be no extension of Community competence in employer–employee relations—the so-called social area. ...

Many of our partners have a wholly different tradition of employment practice which is reflected in the separate arrangements which they have agreed, which will affect only their countries and for which only they will pay. But even among these member states there are many who fear the effect of Community measures on their jobs and their ability to compete. Our arguments are based not only on our national interest but on the risks we perceive to the competitive position of the Community as a whole. ...

Our role has been to put forward practical suggestions—and sometimes to rein in the larger ambitions of our partners. Where we believed their ideas would not work, we have put forward our own alternatives. Those can be found throughout this treaty. As with all international negotiations, there has been give and take between all 12 member states. But the process was one in which Britain has played a leading role, and the result is one in which we can clearly see the imprint of our views. ...

Speech made by John Major to the House of Commons on 20 May 1992 during the second reading of the Bill designed to ratify the Maastricht Treaty

Single Currency

... Clause 2 implements the agreement we secured at Maastricht to ensure that it is entirely a matter for this Parliament to decide whether, and if so when, to join a European single currency. We are under no obligation to do so.

Clause 2 provides that a separate Act of Parliament would be required before the United Kingdom could notify its partners in the Community of its intention to move to the third stage of economic and monetary union. That provision for primary legislation is not a legal requirement which flows from the treaty. It does, however, reflect the Government's belief that it will be for Parliament to determine the issue, and to do so in the way in which Parliament most clearly demonstrates its sovereignty.

I do not believe that it is right to predetermine a decision that should only properly be taken by Parliament, in the light of the circumstances then prevailing across Europe. This decision is too important to be an act of faith—it must also be an act of judgment, and that judgment cannot sensibly yet be made. ...

We have moved decision taking back towards the member states in areas where Community law need not and should not apply.

Subsidiarity

Let me inform those who are unaware of that fact that we have done so in a number of ways. We have secured a legally binding text on subsidiarity. That text provides that any action by the Community shall not go beyond what is necessary to achieve the objectives of the treaty. More specifically, it provides that in areas that do not fall within the exclusive competence of the Community—such as environment, health, education, social policy—the Community shall take action only if and in so far as the objectives of the proposed action cannot be achieved by the member states. ...

We need to ensure that the Commission gives full effect to that requirement. I believe that it is obliged to give full effect to that requirement. Were it not to meet that requirement, we now have the power to take the issue to the European Court of Justice for adjudication. That is a right that we argued for at Maastricht and obtained. ...

Nor does subsidiarity mean that relatively minor issues are returned to the member states in exchange for a growth of power at the centre. I know that that is what many people fear, not least some hon. Members. They fear that the institutions of the Community will increase their powers step by step so that, in the end, we create what we understand by a federal Europe: a strong, central Government in Brussels with some powers devolved to the individual nation state.

I understand those fears, but that is not the route foreshadowed by the Maastricht treaty; nor is it a route down which this country will go. The question is not whether the risk of centralism exists. The question is whether we have the confidence to exert our influence to build the Community we want to see. . . .

Let me explain why I am confident of that. For the first time in a single treaty, agreements between Governments are given equal standing with action under Community law. In foreign and security policy, and in justice and interior matters, the member states will work together when it is in their common interest to do so. What exactly does that mean? It means that, where such co-operation is helpful to this country, we shall co-operate with our partners in Europe. It also means that we cannot be forced into policies we do not approve of. We keep our ability to act on our own where we need to do so. We shall co-operate within a framework of international law but outside the framework of Community law. For example, any dispute would go to the International Court of Justice, not the European Court of Justice. I believe that that marks a vital and important change in direction for the Community. It strengthens the unity of the member states but reinforces the case for tackling our common problems by the most effective means available to us. That may on occasion be the treaty of Rome. It may equally well be intergovernmental co-operation. The Maastricht treaty provides for both, and it allows for neither—where the member states can act better on their own. That opens fresh opportunities for the future development of the Community. . . .

The strength of what we have achieved is not just that the choices that I mentioned a moment ago are in the treaty but, equally important, that they reflect the growing wish of the member states. The old tendency among some of our partners to think that action by the Community was always the answer is diminishing. Many countries joined the Community to strengthen their own national democracy. Now that their own democracy is strong and more firmly rooted, it is becoming much more possible in the Community to have rational discussion about what should be done at Community level and what should be done at national level. That is a healthy development for the future of the whole European Community.

Rule of Law
Within the framework of the Community treaties, we have secured amendments to the treaty of Rome to reflect important United Kingdom objectives. We have strengthened the rule of law in the Community by stricter rules on the implementation of agreed provisions. In future, if directives are agreed across the Community, they must be implemented across the Community, or penalties will inevitably follow. That provision directly responds to the concern felt by many that, while our domestic law compels the United Kingdom to implement Community law speedily, others sometimes do not act with the same dispatch. . . .

Accountability
We have also secured better financial accountability. At Britain's insistence, the Commission will now have to provide an assurance that sufficient resources are available for any proposed Community action. It can no longer commit itself to expenditure for which resources are not available, and we keep a complete lock on the overall resources available to the Community. There can be no increase in those resources unless we agree with our European partners that there should be. There can be no change in our abatement without our agreement, and I have no intention of agreeing to any adverse change in our abatement in the discussions that lie ahead.

The Court of Auditors, which now becomes a Community institution, will present the Council and the European Parliament with a statement of assurance on the reliability of the accounts and the legality of the underlying transactions. The treaty contains new provisions to counter fraud.

In the agreements reached, we have also extended democratic control over the Commission. The European Parliament will in future have authority to call the Commission to account for its expenditure and for the operation of financial control systems. Individuals will be able to petition the Parliament about abuses by any of the Community's institutions. The Parliament will appoint an ombudsman to investigate maladministration by any of the Community's institutions, including the Commission.

Open Market and Frontiers

The treaty also sets exactly the framework that we want for economic and monetary union. It provides a commitment to open and competitive markets, a commitment that this country has sought for years and that many felt might never be available from our Community partners. It sets tough economic tests that any member state wanting to move to stage 3 would have to pass. The framework contains a commitment to price stability. Above all, it contains an absolute right for the United Kingdom—its Parliament—to decide later, and at a time of its own choosing, whether or not it wishes to move to the third stage of economic and monetary union. Those are arguments that we have won in Europe and that set policy in the direction in which we believe it should go. . . .

. . . The future of Europe is . . . based on free trade and competition, on openness to our neighbours, on a proper definition of the limits of the power of the Commission, and on providing a framework for co-operation between member states outside the treaty of Rome. . . .

The concept first put forward, I think, by Ernest Bevin—of being able to buy a ticket at Victoria station and travel freely anywhere in Europe—is attractive. It appeals to the instincts. The freedom to move goods and services lies at the heart of the single market which we British pressed on the Community. But there is a practical problem, recognised in the text of the Single European Act and its accompanying declarations.

All of us in this country live daily with the evils of terrorism and drug smuggling. No one doubts that we have to control immigration, in the best interests of everyone who lives in this country. The issue of the open frontier must be treated rationally, not ideologically. For most of our partners, the idea of an open frontier does not mean that there should be no limitations on what goods and people travel from one country to another. It reflects the fact that they cannot control these matters at the frontier and have therefore devised internal controls to do so.

Our practice is different by virtue of our island status. Experience has shown us that control at the frontier gives us the best possible chance of containing smuggling, terrorism and illegal immigration. We accept the right of Community citizens to move freely between member states, but we must, as we agreed under the Single European Act, keep the controls that we consider necessary to control immigration from third world countries and to combat terrorism, crime and trafficking in drugs. That means that we must retain frontier controls, and we intend to do so. . . .

Community Enlargement

I believe that the developments in the former Soviet Union and across eastern Europe are more significant for the future of the Community than any other development since we joined 20 years ago. By 1995, I hope that Sweden, Austria and Finland will be members. During our presidency, we shall prepare the ground for those enlargement negotiations. By the end of the decade, I hope that Poland, Hungary and Czechoslovakia will have followed suit. Other countries will follow. The Community will have to develop its relationship with the Baltic states and with many of the countries of the former Soviet Union.

The politics, economics and social fabric of the Community will change radically as the Community enlarges. We shall have to show imagination, flexibility and generosity. It would be fatal to take the attitude that we have our prosperous club and that nobody else can join unless they are prepared to pay a heavy price. We—the Community, this country—would all pay a heavy price if, by our attitude, we damaged the chance of re-establishing for the first time in 50 years a firm democracy throughout the whole of Europe.

Some argue that enlargement points to more being done at the Community level. I believe that a Community of 20 member states will need the sort of flexibility that we have shown in the Maastricht treaty. A lot more will have to be done on the basis of intergovernmental co-operation. A lot more may be left to the national level. The changes that we have negotiated do not weaken what is valuable in the treaty of Rome. They do create the flexible framework we need as the Community reaches out to new members. The institutions of the Community must adapt to the needs of the members and not the other way round.

What should not and need not be negotiable are the core beliefs and foundations of the Community: its commitment to democracy, its framework of law, the creation of a genuine single market and the fact that the Community exists to promote the ever closer union of the peoples of Europe.

Conclusion

We in this generation have the opportunity and the responsibility for managing the biggest transition to democracy in our continent in its entire history. There will be many means at our disposal for achieving that, both national and international. I have no doubt that crucial among them is the European Community. If we had to point towards one endeavour that can consolidate European democracy, boost our collective European economic prosperity and enhance our collective international influence, it is the European Community.

Sometimes the national interest and the Community's interests are at variance. Where they are, we shall fight as we have done in the past for our national interest. But I have no doubt that, overall, through the European Community, our national interest can best be promoted. At Maastricht we obtained a good deal for this country. We improved the way in which the Community works. We set the basis for the growth and expansion of the Community in the years ahead. I believe that that was a good deal for this country and for Europe. I invite the House to have confidence in our future in Europe, and to approve the Bill.

Speech made by Neil Kinnock to the House of Commons on 20 May 1992

Support for Treaty

The Labour party has already made it clear that it broadly supports the treaty concluded at Maastricht because it is a necessary framework for the economic, social and political development of the European Community. The treaty provides for majority voting on issues of the environment and on certain other important matters such as youth training and public health. It entrenches the democratic principle of subsidiarity so that decisions are taken at the most appropriate level—local, national or Community. It establishes a cohesion fund and provides for regional policy to be an essential component of the single market. We welcome these changes and we welcome also the fact that the European Parliament is to get new powers that will help to close the democratic deficit caused by the fact that powers and decisions have been ceded to the Commission and other Community institutions. All those and other features of the treaty are worthy of support.

Social Chapter
We cannot, however, extend that support to the Bill. We cannot endorse the Government's action in opting out from the agreements made by the 11 other European Community member countries on social policy and on the approach to economic and monetary union. Both of those decisions by the Government will disadvantage the British people. The social policy opt-out would be reason enough by itself to justify refusal to support the Bill.

Eleven other Community countries—countries with conservative, socialist and coalition Governments—all endorse the social chapter that was agreed at Maastricht. They will all take decisions on social policy on the basis of qualified majority voting on specific matters. The United Kingdom, because of the Government's opt-out, will not be able to vote on those decisions or be part of the deliberations on those decisions. That is not an assertion of sovereignty; it is a resignation of sovereignty.

... The Government refuse to accept the social chapter, which makes provision for qualified majority voting so that the Community can support and complement the activities of member states in 'improvement ... of the working environment to protect workers' health and safety; working conditions; the information and consultation of workers; equality between men and women with regard to labour market opportunities and treatment at work' and the integration into the labour force of the long-term unemployed, including disabled workers. ...

... Whatever else can be said about inferior working conditions, they certainly do not make for superior economic performance. They never have and they never will, and it is high time that the Government faced up to that and stopped hoping that if they can make Britain into the labour market bargain basement of Europe they will have some kind of edge over our competitors. That cannot work and it will not work. That is why the Government's social chapter opt-out is not only an injustice against the British people, but also contradicts Britain's economic interests. Sadly, that is also true of the Government's other opt-out—the economic and monetary union opt-out.

Trade with Community
As the Government come to make their decisions in the near future, uppermost in their minds should be the reality that the European Community has an increasingly interdependent and integrated economy. That is of special relevance and primary significance for our country. Sixty per cent of our exports now go to other EC countries. The leading importer of British goods is Germany. France comes next, and then the United States —which used to take most of our exports. It is closely followed by The Netherlands.

That is the pattern of our trade now and that tendency will increase as we move closer to the single market and the Community is joined by other countries ... and as products and production processes become increasingly integrated in multinational companies.

Given that exports account for one third of our gross domestic product, a large proportion of our production capacity and of British jobs depend on sales in the Community. That basic consideration should guide Government policy on economic and monetary union. The growing interdependence to which I referred will make it essential for the British Government to play a full and constructive role in the process of achieving the economic and monetary union that is under way.

Interdependence
It is not enough for the Government to content themselves with monetary convergence and then to stand back. If only that were on offer, the future would be bleak. Low inflation, low interest rates and manageable levels of public borrowing are all important elements of stability. However, if the Community's future is left at that, the stability achieved could be the stability of stagnation—with continuing high unemployment, low growth, low standards of competitive performance and even worse imbalances between regions.

No member of the Community could benefit from a continuation of such difficulties—which is why it is essential that the Community gives real substance to the task that it defines for itself in article 2 of the Maastricht treaty, of promoting harmonious and balanced development, sustainable and non-inflationary growth, respect for the environment, convergence of economic performance, a high level of employment and social protection, economic and social cohesion and solidarity between member states. ...

It is clear, moreover, that co-ordinated expansion is vital as the most effective antidote to the resentments and tensions that are rooted in economic disadvantage and insecurity. The Maastricht treaty provides a framework for such action. It gives the Council of Economic and Finance Ministers the power and the responsibility to monitor economic performance and it enables the member states and the Council to act as the focus for concerted action. It is an essential basis for the advance that must take place. What is needed now is the willingness to build on that and to see that European countries move forward together. . . .

Within a few weeks, the Prime Minister will become President of the Council of Ministers. He has said that he wants to be at the heart of Europe; that he wants to foster enlargement of the Community; that he wants to reach out to the countries of eastern and central Europe. I put it to the Prime Minister that he can show genuine commitment to those objectives only if he uses his period in the presidency for the purpose of promoting economic expansion and social justice throughout the Community.

Speech made by the Prime Minister, John Major, in the House of Commons on 22 July 1993

Need for Ratification
I believe that ratification of the Maastricht treaty is in the interests of this country. I negotiated the treaty because I believed that it was in the interests of this country, and that is why I signed it. That is why I refused to ditch it or to change it, even though there was plenty of opportunity to do so over the past year. Let me set out to the House the reasons why I regard it as vital for this country, for the reasons do not just relate to what is within the treaty itself, but

go wider than the treaty and relate to the general position in the European Community.

We took the decision to join the Community—the right decision, I believe—over 20 years ago. From the day we took the decision, across both sides of the House, it has often been a matter of controversy. Sometimes it has been bitter, sometimes it has flared up, and at other times, for a while, it has been quiescent. Always that schism between the parties has rested there, and it has damaged the influence than this country has been able to exercise within the European Community.

Too often, as a result of those divisions within this House and sometimes beyond it, this country under successive Governments —I make no party point—has allowed itself and its interests to be sidelined. If it had not been for those disputes, and if we had been able to play the full part in the Community that I believe we should have done, it might not have developed in the way it has, and many of the concerns that some hon. Members have might well have been dealt with.

In that period, we have had many successes in the Community. The British rebate was a great negotiating success. The single market was one of the greatest changes in the EC since its conception. The reform of the common agricultural policy, the enlargement of the EC—each and every one, in its own way, is a big issue that has affected every aspect of the EC. All of them were British successes. It shows that we can win the arguments at the European table. Despite that, we have still not exercised the influence that we should have, or shaped the EC in the fashion that was possible. . . .

Too often over the years, the dominant political attitude has been to object to the ways others have wanted to develop the EC, rather than to set out our plans, our prospects and our hopes and then fight for them to deliver the type of Community that is right for this country.

Many hon. Members are right in their opposition to the way in which the EC operates. Some of the ways that it operates need to be changed—I strongly support that. I want to see the EC reformed, as do my hon. Friends and many Opposition Members, but if we are to reform the EC, Britain must have influence in the EC. We will not have influence if we do not ratify the treaty that we have agreed after consultations in the House.

I did not initiate the negotiations. I have made it clear that I thought that they were premature, and I said so to our partners during our negotiations. I did seek to negotiate what I believed to be the best outcome for Britain. I did so within a remit I had obtained from the House, and after seeking the views of Parliament and negotiating within them.

I believe that, as a result of that discussion and debate within the House, it was right for me to decline to accept the social chapter—and the single currency—without the express will of the House.

I believe that the events which have followed the conclusion of the negotiations have proved that judgment to be correct. As I have told the House before, in my judgment Europe is not yet remotely ready for a single currency, and the present economic circumstances across Europe mean that it cannot afford the ambitions of the social chapter. . . .

If we believe that the social chapter is bad for employment and I do believe that—then it is right for us to argue against it, and to try to persuade our partners to argue against it also.

I believe that that is what we are doing, and increasingly in Europe, businesses and employers are saying what we have said in this country and what I have said from the outset—the charter will destroy jobs across the EC. . . .

Increased British Influence

For the first time in 20 years, we are beginning to see a material move in the European Community agenda in the direction that Britain has long sought. It would be absurd for us to throw away our influence in the Community at this moment. We are seeing enlargement. We are seeing increasing moves towards the repatriation of responsibilities in this country—I hope for concrete progress on that in December. We are seeing proper budget control both within the Commission and right the way across the Community.

The European Community will continue to develop, whatever else may happen. But we need to influence the way of that development and to see that it moves in a way that is congenial to the British interest.

I want a wider European Community. I regard the present Community as but a fragment of Europe. That is why I wish to see the European Free Trade Association countries join, and a little later, our old friends in central and eastern Europe. The wider that we can spread the European Community, with a free market concept not only in economic terms but in military and security terms, the more we shall be able to hand a glorious bonus to the next generation that we should not throw away.

So I want that wider Community—a free-market Community, a Europe with the minimum necessary centralisation, a Europe that exercises more powers through the elected Governments of its member states and fewer powers through unelected commissioners, a Europe in which national Governments exercise undiluted control over genuine domestic policy matters from national elections to our education system, from health care to religion. That is the sort of Community that has been our agenda for a long time, and we are beginning to make progress in encouraging others to support the development of that sort of Community.

We seek a Community that emphasises co-operation between Governments, not imposition from the centre. We seek a Community where member states freely decide the agenda and the outcome. We seek a Community which limits common rules and the jurisdiction of the Court of Justice to matters such as free trade and free competition, where they are genuinely necessary for any level playing field to be established. That is the Community that we seek to develop and shape.

However, we can do that only from the inside. If we are inside the Community fighting for that with allies elsewhere in the Community, we can build properly in the interests of our future. It is a process that we can take much further as a fully committed member of real influence. ...

There is only one way in which we could find ourselves with the centralist, federalist Europe that we do not want, and that would be to sideline ourselves, through our own efforts, and let other nations determine the future development of the Community. That would be a folly of historic proportions for the country and the House. That is why we need to seek allies in the Community, and why we need to honour our obligations and to ratify the treaty that Parliament has approved. ...

Social Chapter
Let me turn directly to the social chapter. Through qualified majority voting—not unanimity—the Community would have the

power to determine social and working conditions. The social chapter would allow the Community to restrict part-time work, whether or not we agreed in this House. It could set a rigid framework for rules and conditions of employment, which would replace the rules developed in this country, and few areas, if any, would be exempt. Trade unions across Europe could forge deals and translate them into Community law, over the heads of individual workers and without the involvement of the British Parliament. ...

Above all, the social chapter would mean that many who are now employed would be likely to become unemployed. Many without jobs would stay without jobs. The main right that workers would get would be the right to become unemployed.

I strongly support our membership of the Community, but I support a Community which does not intrude into areas that are properly the domain of the member states. That, I believe, is what the social chapter does. There is already concern across the House, not just on the Conservative Benches, at the Commission's attempts to use health and safety powers for social legislation. We will oppose any abuse of those powers. ...

Business knows that the Community must compete or contract. If we add to social costs, we will not complete and we shall contract. We shall lose jobs in the short term and the long term. The one certain impact of the social chapter is that jobs will be lost and unemployment will be worse. That is what is at stake. ...

Britain's Voice in the Community
During the past few years, Britain has had an increasingly strong voice in the Community. As never before, we have influenced its future direction. So long as we remain a fully committed member, we can have an even stronger voice in the future.

That does not mean accepting everything wanted by our partners. It means being in there in the Community; arguing, debating, shaping the future of our Community and carrying alliances with us. Europe is beginning to move in our direction. In France, in Germany and in Britain, a large majority looks not to a super-state, not to a united states of Europe, but to a Europe of nation states. Those states co-operate closely and enjoy a single market embracing 340 million people, but they retain their identity and sovereignty....

Britain's interests demand that we play a leading part in the Community. Common sense demands that we retain the freedom of action which I secured in signing the social protocol. That is why the Government are determined to ratify the treaty I signed and to oppose last-ditch efforts to delay or distort it. It is a matter of national interest that we proceed in that fashion, and it is upon that basis that I ask the House to put aside and reject the Opposition amendment, and to adopt the motion.

Speech made by the Leader of the Opposition, John Smith, in the House of Commons on 22 July 1993

... It took the Prime Minister a little while to get round to it, but once again he today advanced the startling proposition that measures of social protection which are thought to be desirable by all 11 of our partner nations in the European Community are in some curious way a threat to British prosperity. ...

Social Protocol

Therefore, it is vital for the House to consider what the social protocol is and what it is not. The other 11 states have agreed that there should be a modest extension of the Community's competence in social affairs—matters such as the protection of the health, safety and working conditions of people at work, workers' rights to information and consultation, and equality for men and women in relation to work opportunities and treatment at the work place. The argument is all about those sectors where qualified majority voting applies.

There are other extensions of competence to social security and social protection where unanimity would still be required. There are sectors—which the Government have consistently failed to acknowledge—which are specifically excluded from the agreement. They include pay, the right of association and the right to strike. ...

I am wholly convinced that adopting the social chapter in this country will improve, rather than undermine, employment opportunities. What is more, I shall develop the argument as I proceed with my speech. ...

In what sense and in what way does the improvement of the working environment to protect workers' health and safety or the improvement of working conditions impede economic growth? How on earth can equality between men and women in labour market opportunities and treatment at work be considered economically harmful in a civilised, modern state? ...

The evidence shows that the member states which embraced the social chapter when Britain rejected it have more impressive records of competitiveness and productivity ... We have no future as the sweatshop of Europe. If we persist in the policies of social devaluation which lie behind the opt-out from the social chapter, I fear that our relative decline will continue. Indeed, it will accelerate.

... Investors at home and abroad today are seeking skills, technology and a highly motivated and self-confident work force. We hear a lot from the Government about inward investment and how that investment would be afraid to come near us if we were to sign up to the social protocol. How strange that in a recent study carried out by Arthur Andersen of Japanese inward investment, wages and social costs are not mentioned by Japanese companies as a factor determining decisions to invest in Britain. The problem which is highlighted and described as most important by Japanese enterprise is 'the difficulty in recruiting skilled or qualified employees'. The Nissan director of personnel gave evidence the other day to the Select Committee on Employment. He dismissed the social chapter as a significant factor in respect of inward investment. ...

I hope that some British companies will copy Nissan, which recently agreed two-year pay deal increases with maternity pay of up to 100 per cent of average earnings for up to a maximum of 18 weeks. Maternity leave has been extended to 40 weeks after birth with existing rights of return to work maintained. Matsushita Electric, Sony and Komatsu have introduced paternity leave for their workers. ...

Far from being put off by the social chapter, the Japanese are ahead of it.

Improved Opportunity

In the real world, the new economic agenda requires a new approach—a positive combination of skills development, decent standards, humane standards, and ever-widening employment opportunities. That must mean giving greater opportunities at work for women on the basis of equal rights and adequate provision for maternity leave and child care—not just because that is their right, but because our economy needs the indispensable contribution that women can make to our future prosperity.

I see the Chancellor of the Exchequer nodding. That is why I find it odd that the Government should object to a social chapter which provides for 'equality between men and women with regard to labour market opportunities and treatment at work'. . . .

I urge the House to vote for the social chapter. It is our responsibility in this House to make the decision and, when we have made the decision, it is the unavoidable responsibility of the Government to accept and to implement what the House has decided.

Further Reading

		£
Britain in the European Community (Aspects of Britain). ISBN 0 11 701712 4.	HMSO	5.50
Treaty on European Union including the Protocols and Final Act with Declarations, Maastricht, 7 February 1992. Cm 1934. ISBN 0 10 119342 4.	HMSO	13.30

EUROPEAN UNION

Abbreviations

ECB	European Central Bank
ECOFIN	Council of Economic and Finance Ministers
ECU	European Currency Unit
EMI	European Monetary Institute
EMS	European Monetary System
EMU	Economic and monetary union
ERM	Exchange rate mechanism
ESCB	European System of Central Banks
NATO	North Atlantic Treaty Organisation
QMV	Qualified Majority Voting
WEU	Western European Union

Index

Agricultural policy 3, 6, 14
Asylum policy 43–4
Austria 2

Bank of England 29
Belgium 2, 5, 6, 7, 41
Britain and:
   accession to European Community 2
   Committee of the Regions 34
   Council of the European Union 5
   economic and monetary union 24, 28–9
   European Commission 6
   European Parliament 7
   exchange rate mechanism 9
   ratification of Maastricht Treaty 46–8
   social dimension 36–8, 47–8
   United Nations 40
   Western European Union 41
Brussels 4, 7, 42
Budget 6, 7, 29–30

Centralisation 12
Citizenship 13, 14, 17–18, 47
Civil protection 15
Cohesion Fund 33
Commercial policy 3, 14, 30
Commission see European Commission
Committee of Central Bank Governors 25
Committee of the Regions 32, 34
Common foreign and security policy 1, 13, 14, 18, 19, 38–43

Consultative committee 21–2
Consumer protection 14, 20, 36
Convergence criteria 26
Council of Europe 2
Council of the European Union 4–6, 7–8, 10, 16, 17, 18, 19, 20, 21–2, 23, 24, 25–6, 28, 29, 31, 32, 33, 34, 35, 36, 37, 39, 40, 41, 43, 44
Court of Auditors 4, 9, 20, 29
Court of First Instance 9, 19, 22
Court of Justice see European Court of Justice
Crime 43–4
Culture 13, 15, 20, 31–2, 34
Customs co-operation 43–4
Customs duties 3, 14

Defence see Common foreign and security policy
Denmark 2, 5, 6, 7, 29, 41, 46–7
Developing countries 3, 13, 14, 36
Drugs 43–4

Economic and monetary union 12, 14, 15, 24–9
Economic policy 15, 23–4
Education 13, 15, 20, 30–1, 34
Employment 37–8
Energy 15, 32
Enlargement 2
Environment 4, 13, 14, 21, 35
European Agricultural Guidance and Guarantee Fund 10
European Atomic Energy Community 2
European Central Bank 24, 27, 28, 29

European Coal and Steel Community 2
European Commission 4, 5, 6, 8, 10, 13, 16–17, 18–19, 21, 22, 23, 24, 25, 26, 29, 31, 32, 35, 37, 38, 39, 40, 43, 44
European Council 3, 5, 7, 10, 12, 14, 16, 24, 26, 27, 46
European Court of Justice 4, 8–9, 13, 16, 19, 22, 38, 44
European Currency Unit 9, 25, 27
European Economic Community 2, 13
European Investment Bank 3, 4, 10, 26
European Monetary Co-operation Fund 9, 25
European Monetary Institute 24–5, 26, 27, 28
European Monetary System 9, 25
European Parliament 4, 6, 7–8, 13, 14, 17, 18–19, 20–23, 26, 29, 30, 33, 34, 35, 41, 44
European political co-operation 11, 38
European Regional Development Fund 10, 33
European Social Fund 3, 9–10
European System of Central Banks 27, 28
Exchange rate mechanism 9, 26

Finland 2
Fishing policy 3, 14
Foreign policy 1, 4, 13, 14, 18, 19, 38–43
France 2, 5, 6, 7, 40, 41, 46
Frankfurt 24
Fraud 29–30, 43–4
Free movement 3, 14, 20, 43

Germany 2, 5, 6, 7, 41, 48
Greece 2, 5, 6, 7, 41

Health and safety at work 37
Health policy 13, 15, 20, 32, 34

Iceland 41
Immigration 43–5
Industry 14, 33
Intergovernmental co-operation 1, 11, 12, 13, 14, 18, 30, 38, 43
Internal market 3–4, 12, 13–14, 26
International agreements 10–11
Irish Republic 2, 5, 6, 7, 41, 46
Italy 2, 5, 6, 7, 41

Justice and home affairs 1, 13, 14, 18, 19, 43–5

Labour affairs 37–8
Luxembourg 2, 4, 5, 6, 7, 41

Membership 2, 8

Negative assent procedure 20–2, 33, 34
Netherlands 2, 5, 6, 7, 41
North Atlantic Treaty Organisation 40, 41, 42–3
Norway 2, 41

Objectives 13–15
Ombudsman 17, 22–3

Paris Treaty (1951) 2
Parliament, European *see* European Parliament
Parliaments, national 23
Police co-operation 43–4
Portugal 2, 5, 6, 7, 41
Qualified majority voting 5, 10, 18, 21, 22, 23, 24, 25, 26, 27, 31, 32, 34, 35, 36, 39, 44

Ratification of Maastricht Treaty 46–8
Referendums 46
Regional policy 9–10, 33–4
Research and development 4, 14, 21, 34–5
Rome Treaty (1957) 2, 3, 10, 12, 13, 18, 37

Single European Act 2, 3–4, 5, 11
Social policy 36–8, 47–8
Spain 2, 5, 6, 7, 41
Strasbourg 4, 7
Structural Funds 9–10, 33
Subsidiarity 12, 15–17, 18
Sweden 2

Telecommunications 32
Tourism 15
Trade 3, 6, 10, 14, 15
Training 13, 15, 31, 37
Trans-European networks 15, 20, 32–3, 34
Transport 14, 32
Turkey 41

United Nations 39, 40

Visa policy 44–5
Voting *see* Qualified majority voting

Western European Union 40, 41–2
World Health Organisation 32

Printed in the UK for HMSO.
Dd.0297719, 4/94, C30, 56-6734, 5673.